F

)

—

WITHDRAWN

Mr ALBION

by

Dave Matthews

Thomas Publications

First published in Great Britain in November, 2013
by Thomas Publications, 26 Park End,
Newport, Shropshire, TF10 7JG
Reprinted in December, 2013

ISBN 978-0-9550585-6-1

Thomas Publications

Printed and bound by TJ International, Padstow, Cornwall

Contents

This book is dedicated to the memory of
David Malcolm Matthews, 'Dave', and to all family,
friends, players and colleagues who made it possible.

Preface

This should have been an autobiography. Correction: It is an autobiography; at least it is for the most part. Tragically, at 67, Dave passed away suddenly at home while watching Match of the Day 2 one Sunday night in April, having evidently beaten cancer. The West Bromwich Albion family were stunned and hugely saddened. Only the day before, he had attended his final football match and was planning to go to another in the midweek. He was doing well. Football friends enthused over how he was looking considering the illness that had kept him off work during the last of his 51 years at The Hawthorns. They shared the belief that he would have a long and happy retirement, surrounded by his loving family and contented with his hobbies. The biggest grumble he voiced when greeted with cheery observations from those he hadn't seen for a while was over his hip, which he was considering having replaced.

The devastation I felt when informed of Dave's death was followed by an assumption that the many happy days we had spent on this project would have to be written off as just that; happy days. My early reaction was that the book wouldn't see the light of day without his continued input and this would remain one of the great untold Albion stories. On the very day the awful news came through from his wife Carol, though, I also received the first of a series of calls and emails imploring me to see the publication through. "Dave was such a top bloke.......we'll help you finish it" was the gist of the messages. Maybe that half a century's worth of anecdotes, memories and unique fly-on-the-wall insight would see the light of day after all....

Clearly, nothing would have been possible, or ethical, by way of continuation without the approval of Dave's lovely family; namely Carol and daughters Alison, who spent around ten years as the secretary to a string of managers at Albion, and Clare. But one of them let it be known to me at The Hawthorns on the day of the funeral in early May that there was a desire to carry on. And the other two immediately confirmed when asked discreetly that they were of the same mind. Clare went a step further and said the book would be a fitting 'final tribute.' We all recognise it as a crying shame that Dave won't see the finished article but, equally, that this is what he would have wanted. Remarkably, he had been working on his life story for 12 years or more, since

February 2001, and made the point over and over again in a catalogue of diaries going back to the mid-1980s that he had an autobiography on his mind. Those personal volumes have been constant companions to me over recent months and, as if they weren't enough by way of material, he also recorded his thoughts on around a dozen cassette tapes. He really wanted this book done.

I became involved as his ghost-writer only in the summer of 2011, after which he and I twice had full days of memory-jogging at the family home in Halesowen and met on other occasions at the Novotel in Wolverhampton, the Holiday Inn at Great Barr, the Park Inn near The Hawthorns, the former players' golf day at Walsall – even one hot summer's afternoon at the factory in Middlemore Lane at which the miniature model of the Three Degrees statue was being shown off. He was a prime supporter of Jim Cadman's ambitious plan to have a permanent memorial erected to Laurie Cunningham, Cyrille Regis and Brendon Batson in West Bromwich town centre, immediately making it clear he would channel a percentage of the proceeds to the fund when he auctioned off his massive collection of signed memorabilia. Jim recalls that he was, in fact, the first person to step forward with an offer of help.

Dave and I also had two long sessions with former managers, one of three hours at Ron Atkinson's home in February and one that stretched to five with Tony Mowbray and his assistant Mark Venus at their Black Country hotel before a game at Wolves in mid-March. That was the last time Dave and I met. By April, we had done around 75 per cent of the work, hence the reason why some of the text near the end of the book appears in the third person, rather than the first. This was the publishers' way of filling in the gaps that remained. Another important issue still on our 'to do' list at the time of Dave's passing was deciding on a title. 'Kit-Man Dave' was rejected as being adequate but uninspired, 'Get Your Kit Out For The Lads' was deemed too blokey for a man with two respectable grown-up daughters and 'Fifty Shades Of Navy' was promising, tantalising even, but not necessarily appropriate enough in identifying the content. We were even considering 'Read It In The Book' – a nod to the default response Dave gave to a number of colleagues who asked him for a certain inside track on Albion stories over the decades. One of the other options is discussed by Dave in his Introduction but it is one that was felt just didn't do him justice.

Then, quite late in the day, the penny dropped. At the dinner to celebrate his magnificent 50 years' service and in an Express & Star article around the same time, Ron Atkinson referred to his loyal, long-standing friend – he was more than just another work mate – as Mr Albion. That tag rang the appropriate bells when it was repeated on a relative's beautiful wreath carried behind the coffin on that sunny but desperately sad early-May day. The funeral write-up on Albion's website and the headline on Tom Ross's column in the Birmingham Mail used the same term to refer to him. Decision made. Dave would have been embarrassed at being adorned with that title, of course, and would have insisted it belonged to the Tony Browns of this world. Modesty would have seen to that. But here is a man – a Baggies fan as a boy, no less – who has served the club hands-on for half a century and clocked up well over 2,500 games in the process. He's Mr Albion, all right.

Thank-you to everyone who gave us the encouragement to continue with this fitting and now posthumous tribute when it might well have been sidelined. Dave had a wonderful story to tell – he was a confidante, agony aunt even, to so many players over the years, after all – and we're delighted to have been the ones able to help him tell it. And we trust there's a highly popular, loyal club servant looking down proudly from the sky as the cherished end product hits the shelves.

David Instone

Foreword

I was the last Albion player to speak to Dave Matthews. The day before he died, we exchanged texts after he saw my photo in the programme at the Wolves game he was attending. Actually, we exchanged insults because that's what we did. He would have been calling me a long-haired Scottish so and so who had swapped the navy blue and white in the 1980s for the gold and black of the fierce rivals down the road. I would have been having a right go back and reminding him that he didn't know what he was talking about when, alongside John Wile, he chose John Kaye (my first Baggies hero and a man who to this day I will never allow to buy the drinks when we meet) ahead of me in his best Albion side from the last 50 years. Good mates can get away with comments like that.

After a reporter rang me for my thoughts on the unbelievable news that Dave had passed away, I started to think about all those barbed messages and hoped he had deleted them. I needn't have worried. His widow, Carol, thanked me for the banter between the two of us and said he had loved it, especially during the challenges of his illness when his spirits had needed lifting. Match days were when the fans saw us at work but Dave and me had been close colleagues five or six days a week for almost two decades. And, Monday to Saturday, 40 odd weeks a year, we laughed and giggled away in that dressing room when the game or the training session was over. On the pitch and in the face of criticism, footballers fight and stick up for one another. Behind closed doors, they are ruthless with their mickey-taking and find humour in the daftest things.

I was at The Hawthorns for 18 years and Tony Brown played there for even longer than that. When you think we could have doubled that length of service and still been nowhere near the time Dave Matthews served the Albion, you realise just how loyal he was. In the 1960s and 1970s, he was in effect the boss to any number of home-grown lads, like Bomber, Asa Hartford, Len Cantello, Bryan Robson, Derek Statham and myself, that came through to be Baggies stalwarts. I was a good lad and did my work off the field as well as on it but he was hard and on top of you in making sure you did. I actually helped him with the kit at our Spring Road training ground in the days when we just hung it up to air at the end of a sweaty day rather than send it to be washed. Others swept the dressing room, worked outside at the stadium or cleaned the boots. If he thought you needed bringing down a peg or two, he would order you to clean the toilets.

There was a hierarchy. You respected the senior players and the staff who were in charge. Nobody took the mick more than Jeff Astle but when I was rewarded for some decent performances in the reserves by being taken along for the ride to a first-team game at Newcastle, he had me at his side as his 'banker' in the card school. He was the loveliest man and wanted you involved. This was our upbringing at The Hawthorns, our path to being a fully fledged member of the first-team squad. Dave Matthews was at the centre of this progression. He lived with us through the good times and the bad and was very much inside the 'bubble' that was the dressing room or team coach. If you had a bad game, he bit his tongue or said something that would give you a little lift. If you had a good game, he would say something like: "I'm told you did a bit better on Saturday......" He always tried to keep your feet on the ground. But he respected those who did their best and, once you were starting to make the grade and leaving your L plates behind, he was great.

He could have been dangerous because he saw and heard everything. At times, we told him so much and, if the wrong things had got back to the manager, we would have been in trouble. But we confided in him because we trusted him and that trust was never abused. He was the perfect buffer between the players and the gaffer. Here's a confession as well: We took him for granted. A good kit-man will just have your gear there every day for training or matches and be ready to meet any emergency with replacement bits and pieces. Okay, I don't have much sense of perspective here because Wolves were on their knees when I first got there and their staff was cut right back to the bone, but Dave was a very, very good kit-man.

He must have saved the club a fortune by stitching up boots that were falling apart. And he did it without moaning or groaning. He just got on with his job, day after day, for 51 years. He did it because he loved the Albion and I don't know anyone who has ever had a bad word to say about him. This bit didn't make it on to any of those texts but what a lovely man he was!

Alistair Robertson

Introduction

For The Love Of The Shirt

My ghost writer reminds me that no-one has been present for more dressing-downs in the Albion dressing-room than me; nor been in the dug-out at more Baggies matches. It obviously follows that no man has travelled on the coach to anything like the number of matches that I have or worked closely with as many managers here. That's 26 by the way, starting with Gordon Clark and ending with the current England boss Roy Hodgson. Something else I can say without any fear of contradiction is that I hold a place in Hawthorns history for putting the famous stripes on the backs of so many of those great and not so great players over six different decades. Fred Everiss and his son Alan each served the club for around 50 years but I don't suppose the half century of employment I have now signed off from will ever be matched again. I've been in a privileged position. People used to ask if I ever planned to get a proper job, especially fans who considered my life 'on the inside' at Albion a privilege they would pay for. I even toyed with the idea of using a variation on that remark and making the title of this book something like: 'Fifty Years – And Never Had A Proper Job.'

It wasn't only managers, players and administrative staff that came and went while I stayed. From the back garden of my parents' house, I could see the original floodlights being erected in the 1950s and watched much closer up as they were dismantled in the 1990s. The distinctive scoreboard in the Woodman Corner came down, too. In 2004, with demolition complete and preparation for the construction of the East Stand under way, I was heard to remark: "Now the Rainbow Stand has been knocked down, I'm the oldest thing left here." Certainly I'm long enough in the tooth to have seen and done such a lot. One of the kit-men at Ipswich drove the coach as well and later became their stadium manager. I did a few hours of service at the wheel en route to a first-team game as well and that appears in this book as one of the multitude of stories I have assembled. Another concerns my ban from the coach for a supposed misdemeanour concerning the directors. I also played a couple of games in emergency for the A team in the Midland Intermediate League and once served as physio on trips to Scandinavia and the Far East. But I was generally happiest when my role was understated and very much behind the scenes. That was enough for me.

Tony Mowbray used the phrase that a good kit-man is barely seen. He referred to how players and staff turning up for training each day, or for matches, just get used to seeing their gear hanging on the right peg. So 'Fifty Years And Hardly Seen' was another title I considered. But I'll explain briefly why I considered another one even more strongly. I lost count of the number of times players would sidle over to me and tell me that their son's school had got a fete coming up, or how there was a Sunday team near them who had had their kit stolen and had a big cup final that weekend. They knew I had the keys to the kit cupboard and they were on the scrounge. But I made a habit of cutting them short in their tracks by emphasising: "The answer's 'No!'" For a particularly good cause, like Darren Moore's charity work, or at the end of a season, I would sometimes relent. But the lads must have got fed up of me digging my heels in. "I've got to account for all this lot and if shirts and shorts go missing, the board will be asking me why," was my stock reply. In a TV interview, Scott Carson apparently said of me: "His favourite word was 'no'." The players will know they had to make a strong case if they wanted giveaways!

This is MY story; a kit-man's story; the account of how I basically helped dress Albion players for work for more than 50 years. Other people are much better qualified than me to comment on the abilities of the players and managers I've known here, so I have kept critical analysis of their efforts – whether they were good or bad – to a minimum. But nobody has had the privilege of the extended fly-on-the-wall view I've had here through so many ups and downs. In these pages, I hope I have successfully opened the window on what was my world and allowed you a good look inside. I even taped, with his permission of course, Gary Megson's stirring pre-match address to the players before the promotion-clinching win over Crystal Palace in 2002. We have played it back in recent months and it's revealing stuff, I promise. Read it and you'll realise why the Wolves never had a chance of beating us to the Premier League that day.

I overlooked the possible use of one ghost writer when he enthused over the prospect of me having so much scandal to expose. He may have been making the comment tongue in cheek but I didn't want my autobiography to be rattling too many skeletons in the cupboard. Yes, there are accounts of a few barneys – not to mention a whole lot of strange goings-on like the player who deliberately kicked balls into the crowd where his mate bagged them up and took them away – but the story is much more about my take on the personalities I worked with and the ups and downs we lived through together; it's the tale of how a quiet Smethwick boy grew up to work for half a century for the club he loved. And how the job changed beyond all recognition in the process.

One thing I can't be accused of is deciding on the spur of the moment to write a book. For decades right back to the 1980s, I kept diaries and decided about 12 years ago that I would one day have my autobiography published. I was certainly putting feelers out for someone to help me around the time we first won promotion to the Premier League in 2002 and I thank David Instone for finally stepping into the role. From the time we first met over coffee in the Merry Hill Centre two or three years ago while our wives were on separate shopping expeditions, I knew his writing and publishing experience was what I needed to turn this wish into reality. I trust there's something in these pages for ALL Albion fans, such as an outline of some of the unusual ways I used to supplement my income in the earlier days. Well, I can assure you the explosion in players' wages didn't filter down to the kit room. But what a way it was to earn a decent living! I saw loads and heard loads and, as I was frequently reminded, I became by far the oldest surviving 'fixture' at The Hawthorns.

Chapter One

Young And Impressionable

I'm sure the many Albion players who moaned at me down the years for not letting them have bits of kit as presents, raffle prizes or just as souvenirs should have blamed my mom and dad. I was a war baby, or near enough, and the careful ways that were an essential part of life at that difficult time rubbed off on me without a doubt. There were no football millionaires then and the average working-class family had to scrimp and save to get by. I was born on November 6, 1945. A look back in the record books reminds me it was a Wednesday in between two handsome Albion victories over Millwall (by 3-1 and 4-1) in the Football League South. The sport was just getting back on its feet after the suspension of competition as fans knew it and players like Ike Clarke, Billy Elliott and the up-and-coming Ray Barlow and Len Millard were pulling on those baggy shorts and famous blue and white stripes. My dad was a fan but not a huge one, which was just as well. I don't think he could ever have afforded to make more than the occasional trip to games. He was a tool setter in Rolfe Street in Smethwick and hated his working life. It was all about greasy hands and he didn't want me following him into a factory. My older brother Frank shared more than the same Christian name with him. He also inherited his love of mechanics, so maybe there wasn't pressure for visits to The Hawthorns.

My schools were George Betts Junior in Smethwick and Smethwick Hall Boys. That latter establishment was for those who failed their 11 plus. I didn't do well in mine. I think I got my name and address wrong. It was pure nerves – I'd like to think I was cleverer than my paper showed. Our school didn't churn out academic wizards but I wasn't a complete no-hoper. I got my bronze in the Duke of Edinburgh award scheme and, as one of my activities, I built a canoe, which I sailed on the lake in Stony Lane, next to the school. Metalwork, woodwork and sport seemed to be the cornerstone of our education.

Naturally, like many lads, I allowed myself a few dreams of being a footballer and had a sort of taste of the kit that would play such a big part in my life when I pulled on the stripes at an early age. Unfortunately, it was the green and white variety (the strip chosen by the school) rather than the navy and white. We used a pitch in West Smethwick Park and I was selected in goal for a while. I moved to full-back because I was accused of not diving around enough. Dad used to come and watch on Saturday mornings without telling me. I never wanted him there. We lived in Bowden Road in a terraced property with a garden. Ronnie Allen's house was at the top in the continuation of it, Frank Road. The houses are still there. Derek Kevan stayed in digs round the corner in Marion Road and Jack Bannister lived there as well. Later, Micky Fudge, a cheerful Bristol lad who didn't quite fulfil his promise despite scoring a hat-trick against Everton, and Tony Brown had digs in Smethwick. Bomber's were in Norman Road and Lyndon Hughes was also from there. The unrelated Lee Hughes grew up in the area as well much later.

Watching the Hawthorns floodlights going up in the second half of the 1950s was exciting as Albion hadn't had them before. Not many clubs had. Each few days, the pylons grew a bit taller. We could also see the roof above the Smethwick End terrace. I had a taste for football but didn't play it in the garden. There were too many flower beds and it wasn't big enough. So our kick-abouts were in the street and up in West Smethwick Park, where games went on virtually until total darkness fell. We would re-enact the previous Saturday's match and I was happiest pretending I was Ronnie Allen or Ray Barlow. Ronnie was a hero to every football-loving youngster then and Ray was another star in my eyes. He would be in or very close to my all-time best Albion team. I once had a pair of his suede boots, gorgeous and soft, and used to play in them in the Sunday League. I'm guessing they were probably left in the boot room when he joined Birmingham and I had them for a few years. I was the best turned out player in the division and regret mislaying them. More than likely, I did what I nagged hundreds of apprentices about in later seasons and left them dirty. They would have gone mouldy and my mum probably threw them out.

The first game I recall seeing was the 1954 FA Cup final between Albion and Preston. We hadn't got a TV, so we watched it on a small black and white set at the home of my dad's work-mate very near Winson Green prison. I remember there was a cuckoo clock that proved a bit of a distraction as it went off every half-hour during Albion's epic 3-2 win. Ronnie's two goals made sure my hero worship of him grew stronger that day, although it was Frank Griffin who had the room in raptures by hitting the winner near the end. There were half a dozen of us crowded around, the more enlightened (in other words, the older ones) all offering insight with shouts of 'Man on' or 'Shoot' at the appropriate times. That game whetted my appetite and cemented other favourites in my mind, like the left-winger George Lee. He was working for the club a few years later after I had been taken on and we were painting the dressing rooms at the end of one season, with me on a plank between two ladders while George was painting a ceiling. I asked: "Where I shall put this pot of paint where it won't get knocked over." He replied: "Down here by my right foot. I've never kicked anything with that." He wasn't always so sure, though. He once slipped down a ladder and bruised and skinned his shins on the rungs. I got on well with George and was sorry when he moved on to Norwich.

I wish I could remember who Albion were playing when I first went to see them live. All I know is I hadn't reached my teens and started going with mates like Martin Penn, Graham Lowe, Graham Guest and Tony Eades. We would stand on the Brummie Road End, taking advantage of the railway sleepers which created the steps leading up to the terrace. There was also a wooden hut where they sold Bovril and lovely rich fruit cake – what a mixture! Try getting that combination past the nutritionists who are everywhere in the game now. I also remember standing behind the goal in a crowd of well over 50,000 at the famous match against the Russian Red Army in 1957. It was the game staged to commemorate the switching-on of the Hawthorns floodlights. A prestige fixture I missed was Norman Heath's testimonial against an International XI which pulled in over 55,000. The TV celebrity Sabrina kicked it off and Bobby Robson pleased the photographers by carrying her off with a flourish. I reminded him of the occasion in his final years when we played at Newcastle and he replied: "How could I forget that?"

Grounds were very different then. Home and away fans mingled without any problems and youngsters were passed over the heads of adults at big games, so they could sit on the track round the pitch if there was a danger of crushing. Look in the record books to see how huge the crowds were for some cup games, especially. We had 53,000 in the quarter-final at home to Arsenal in 1957, over 58,000 against Nottingham Forest the year after and nearly the same for the visit of Manchester United a few weeks after the Munich air crash. I was lucky to grow up watching Albion when they were one of the best teams in the country. The 1954 Cup winners would have lifted the League title as well – and so become the first winners of the double in the 20th century – if they hadn't fallen away over the final games and been beaten to the prize by Wolves. Villa and Blues also reached cup finals over the following few years in what was a wonderful time for West Midlands football.

I also used to go to the reserve games and, in the interests of saving pocket money for something else, would wait until they opened the gates for the last 20 minutes. If I remember right, that's how I caught a glimpse of the Villa v Wolves FA Cup semi-final at The Hawthorns in 1960. One of my first football memories is hearing about the Munich air crash and feeling so sad because I had seen Manchester United lose 4-3 here not long before. Watching them perform underlined through my young, impressionable eyes what everyone was saying: that they were going to be a really great team. I was well aware of Matt Busby's philosophy with his 'babes' but the same players seemed to play for years at Albion once they broke through. Derek Kevan used to watch me play for the school team in the park on a Saturday morning and I watched him play in the afternoon for Albion for several seasons. You can imagine the pride I felt when my working routine partly entailed getting kit ready for The Tank to go and scare opposition defenders to death. I broke down at his funeral earlier this year when 'You'll Never Walk Alone' was being sung and two members of the family stood up at the front and told us all to get on our feet and join in. Derek had run the Ansells Social Club at Perry Barr after retiring and I'd go there and have a drink once a week or so with a couple of mates and see his two lovely dogs. It was sad he got in trouble with the tax man and had to sell a lot of possessions, even his furniture.

What a character Derek was! Graham Williams tells the story about how Derek and Alec Jackson were late for training one Monday because they had spent a weekend back in Yorkshire and had to turn back when Derek realised en route he had left his teeth behind. Tony Brown describes him as his first Albion hero and Derek was among my favourites as well. God knows how many times I got his signature. Football-crazy as I was, I would go with mates to collect autographs at games – including those at Villa, Blues and Wolves when I was a bit older – and even went to the station to greet visiting teams as they stepped off the train. Derek's signature was always one of the most prized.

When I was approaching leaving day at school, carpentry, decorating and gardening were in my head as possible careers. As a hopeful full-back, I'd had a trial with the county at about 15 but went no further and knew I wasn't good enough to be another Len Millard or Stan Rickaby. My uncle was a keen carpenter and made a living from it. Dad didn't want me to go in a factory and I didn't want to sit behind a desk, so he suggested that I used my interest in gardening and tried to find a job on the groundstaff at Albion. If I wasn't good enough to play on that lovely expanse of grass, perhaps I could cut it instead. I left school at Christmas but my mom Mary, who was a twin, had had operations on her feet because of the condition known as hammer toes and was in plaster cast shoes. I did the shopping until she was more mobile and took some of the strain with the housework. She had had a toe removed from each foot and her recovery slightly delayed my entrance into the working world. But Dad contacted the Albion secretary Alan Everiss and was told there was a position available in helping Harry Ashley with the kit, although not one working on the upkeep of the ground. Being shown round the dressing rooms by Alan as part of my interview raised my interest and I knew I'd be well placed for pitch duties if I was engaged by the club when a post came up. I still wasn't sure it was really what I wanted but I decided to give it a whirl and see how it went.

Chapter Two

Among My Heroes

It was January, 1961, when I started work at Albion as a shy but polite 15-year-old. I was on £2.50 a week, paid on a Thursday or Friday in a brown envelope. We had to go to the window at reception and sign for it. My first League game as a member of the British workforce featured the same two clubs as the first match I remember seeing on TV, Albion and Preston North End. The sense of coincidence didn't stop there. Albion, with Gordon Clark as manager, won this one as well by scoring three times. I wasn't the only new boy. Clive Clark had just been signed for £17,000 from Queens Park Rangers and lined up that day for the first of his 350 or so games on our left wing. What a handful he was to opposition full-backs.

I think I was just lucky that a job was available when I needed one. I was delighted to know I was going to be working with my heroes. I was actually overawed to start with and found myself tongue-tied in the company of the senior players. If I knew they were in the dressing room, I wouldn't go in. They used to tell me I was always smiling and I replied meekly: "Yes, that's because I'm here working with you." For a year or two, I used to get the home and away teams to sign every programme. I was a bit freer then as I was assisting Harry and had some free time on a match day. I sold the programmes at an auction a few years ago. My first duties were scrubbing boots and cleaning kit in the wash room. I was based at The Hawthorns because the training ground was nothing like the spick and span complex the club have these days just off the A34 near Great Barr. Fifty years ago, the players did most of their preparation and practice a mile or so from the stadium at Spring Road – a facility that attracted its fair share of fame thanks to two big Albion stories early in that decade; the players' strike over Jimmy Hagan's decision to ban them from wearing tracksuit bottoms even in the coldest of weather, and the disappearance of his car down a deep bank and into the canal. I am assured the two events were completely unconnected.

Strike action was being talked of at the time of my arrival as well. A players' walk-out across the country was threatened in a dispute over freedom of contract but thankfully matches continued and we won at Burnley in the first away match after I was taken on. Another lad called Selwyn Vale was helping with the kit as well. He was from West Bromwich and was on the club's books as an amateur. He featured among a cast of dozens on one of the first squad pictures Tony Brown appeared on. The club couldn't decide whether to take Selwyn on, so he did the kit in the mornings and then trained in the afternoon, as well as playing on a Saturday in the third team. There were half a dozen sides then. Eventually, he learned that he was not going to be given a contract and he played instead in the Southern League for Hereford, where Colin Addison got to know him.

The Hawthorns was a magical place in my impressionable eyes and I clearly remember the lay-out of the old Halfords Lane main stand. Going in through the players' door, the visitors' dressing room was on the right and the home one on the left. The away team's facility was quite small and had one toilet and a large deep bath with a brass tap. There was a staff room right outside the home dressing room, which was L-shaped and had a toilet, bath with a huge brass tap, showers and a big round basin in the middle of the room. The referees' room was along the corridor and was neat, tidy and narrow. It had a cabinet with whisky, brandy, sherry, beer, mixers, tea, sandwiches and fruit cake. The officials were well looked after, although I trust they left the alcohol untouched until after the game. The boiler house (with an oil-fired boiler) was on the left. Also nearby were the kit room, drying room (where the players would go to get a sweat on if they needed to shed a pound or two), boot room, programme office and treatment room. There was a door off the boot room which led into the shareholders' bar and that was lined with old pictures, such as of the FA Cup finals Albion had played in. We had a crate of oranges and apples every week. I had one piece of fruit a day and there was a drink of orange juice and glucose, which I can taste now. It was absolutely fabulous. I used to make it after training on a Friday if the lads were at The Hawthorns. They couldn't get enough of it. The dressing room had plants in it and bowls of fruit after training every day, even Brylcreem. I'd guess that it was very forward-looking for the time.

Eventually, the visitors' changing facilities were moved down to where the treatment room, programme office and boot room were. The treatment room went where the staff room and part of the dressing room had been. A bigger entrance area was developed, with a bit of a glass front and seats for people to wait. Directly opposite the home dressing down towards the Smethwick End was an oak-panelled VIP room. By that was the inner sanctum – the directors' match-day room. You could smell the wood and find yourself marvelling at how old some of the fixtures and fittings were. There was also a kitchen and ladies' tea room while Alan Everiss had an oak-panelled office and there were rooms for the groundsman and for the storage of kit and towels. The arrangements were changed after Don Howe came back from Arsenal in 1971 as manager. The drying room was turned into a proper kit room and cupboards were erected in the corridor, so a lot more space was created for me. Alan Everiss was a very efficient secretary. If he asked a question, he didn't like you to say: "I think so." He'd tell you to go back and see him when you were sure.

My first boss Harry Ashley was the original skinhead. He shaved his hair off to make him look even tougher than he was. He'd grab young groundstaff lads by the sideburns if a ticking-off was called for. He had a right set-to once with one of the young players, and Bobby Hope, who was only 16 when he made his debut against Arsenal just before I was taken on, tells me that Harry thought nothing of clouting a young lad round the back of the head if he stepped out of line. You couldn't do that now. There was a little 'previous' between Harry and me. When I was still a schoolboy, I'd be at The Hawthorns on training days two or three times a week during holidays, hoping for a glimpse of my heroes and the chance to get some autographs. We'd sneak into the ground to watch them if they were running round the pitch and he'd yell: "Go on, clear off!" He had played for Albion but not in the first team and was a local guy with a strong Black Country accent. He may have been strict and not prepared to stand any nonsense from cheeky whipper-snappers but he was fair. If I asked for time off – maybe to go and watch an away game – he always tried to be accommodating. He was good like that.

Selwyn and me thought we were in trouble when Harry told us to run a bath for the manager Gordon Clark and put soda crystals in. We poured in a whole bucketful and he wasn't the only one hopping around after developing a certain burning sensation. We were like cats on a hot tin roof as well waiting for the inevitable inquest and agreed to blame one another. We didn't hang around long enough to ask Gordon how uncomfortable it was, nor did we ever let on that we'd overdosed him. Somehow, we got away with it but it taught us to be more careful in future. Much of what else we were taught came from Harry. He showed me how to lace the balls so they weren't dangerous to head and also how to insert a new bladder in them. I've still got the tools here that I used in the days before the valve came in as the only means of ensuring the ball remained inflated. He also used to send me round to the café owned by the former Albion player Ted Sandford by where the Woodman Pub stood for many years next to the ground. My job was to take tickets for the customers, including some for a gentleman who eventually became chairman. Harry was a jack of all trades. Every month, he had to strip down the oil-fired boiler and dressed for the task in his gown, mask and wellies.

The studding of all the boots was something else he did but I'd help him brush them off after training and games and make sure the players' day-by-day kit – t-shirt, shorts, and woolly green-blue Army ankle socks – were placed in a sack and put to dry overnight. Each player's bag had his initials on. The kit was often just dried and probably went to the laundry twice a week, three times maximum if the weather demanded it. Not like now, when it's done every day. If the oil-fired boiler went down, damp kit would have to be worn next day. The players had towels as well with the club's name embroidered in them and their initials marked on. The washing was done about half a mile away at the Co-op Laundry near the corner of Camp Lane, where the cemetery is. The girls would wait on a Friday and ring to ask where the training kit was because they had an eye on the clock with weekend approaching. Ours would be the last laundry in but they were Albion fans, so they cut us some slack with the deadlines. One of my chores was to gather the kit as soon as the players stepped out of it so it could be rushed to the washer women. Things haven't changed, because someone might be having a massage or treatment or would want shooting practice or to play head tennis. I had to wait until they had finished before collecting it. There was no point going off with two-thirds of it and having to make a second trip with the rest. The revolting garments would be washed, dried and pressed, then taken down to the far end of the laundry building to be folded and parcelled in brown paper or a wicker basket, so I could pick them up, all clean and fresh, on the Friday teatime. With that routine, everything would be ready for the players again on the Monday.

From match days, home or away, the dirty kit would be left in the drying room for the weekend, maturing nicely for when I got in on a Monday. I took it to the Co-op in the A35 van the club had bought, having learned to drive behind the wheel of a tractor at the club and somehow passed my test first time. Harry couldn't drive, so I came in useful with that task. The socks went to Mrs Beckett, Alan Everiss's mother-in-law. She was like old Mother Riley and hand-scrubbed them after they were delivered to her house at Carters Green on a Saturday night. She got them cleaner than the laundrette could. Harry would get things ready for the games, including hanging the kit on the pegs, and leave the day-to-day training gear to me. He'd spend ages on a Friday morning cleaning and checking boots and building the leather up. The studs in those days tended to be a leather screw-in rather than a nailed-in one. For more difficult repairs, we used the cobblers in West Brom, Paynes, but I eventually took them to Ivor Simkins' in Halfords Lane. Although he's now retired, Ivor has continued to do some repairs as well as stitching at home and we have his stitching machine at the ground. Players' footwear used to have more patch on them than original boot. Present-day players don't bother with repairs. They get given so many boots by manufacturers that they can throw them away at the first scratch and put on a brand new pair.

In icy weather, steps were taken to give the lads extra grip by exposing the nails that held the stud in. These were surrounded with wax for when the referee came in to inspect the boots but the players would rub their feet on the concrete when they were in the tunnel so they were showing again. It was a tough game, that's for sure. Harry Ashley and Alan Everiss weren't the only characters or figures of authority in my formative years. Fred Pedley was the physio who gave flu and tetanus injections – and shook like a leaf in the process. He had a tipple before he got to work on vaccinating us, just to steady his hand. That's what he said anyway.

Gordon Clark soon departed to be replaced by Archie Macaulay, who was known as The Scarlet Pimpernel. He was hardly ever there. As a Scot, he used to enjoy his whisky and I think he became a driving instructor or traffic warden in later life. Archie might have found himself some business while he was in charge because not many players drove in. As top dog, Ronnie Allen did have a car and I was delighted he was there when I started and disappointed when he went off so soon to join Crystal Palace. Most of the others came on the bus and Bobby Robson and his big mate Dave Burnside famously used to kick a ball to each other or play one-twos off the wall as they ran in from their digs in Handsworth. Alec Jackson, whose face used to go bright red when he trained in hot weather, opted for his bike. Chuck Drury stuck with public transport and once said he was late because his hat blew off just as he was getting on a bus. He got away with it but wouldn't have done so in Kevin Campbell's time here after the turn of the century. Kevin was in charge of fines for many of the squad's minor misdemeanours and would have had a field day with an excuse like that.

I used to cycle in to work or walk if I had plenty of time. And if there were a few spare minutes in the work day, I would play cricket with Selwyn. There was also a snooker room with a coal fire near the Smethwick End corner. As I gained a little much-needed confidence, the chance to socialise came along and I remember going to the Blue Gates pub in Smethwick High Street with the players and staff for a Christmas meal during Major Keys' time as chairman. My first two years or so were fairly low-key on the pitch as we remained a comfortable top-flight club who were unable to reproduce the FA Cup heroics of the 1950s. But exciting, turbulent times were round the corner.

Chapter Three

Hold Tight, Here's Hagan

Jimmy Hagan was Jekyll and Hyde, chalk and cheese. As a football man, he was strong-willed, knew what he wanted and led by example. Away from the game, he was gentle and funny. I was lucky to see both sides of him after he arrived from Peterborough in the spring of 1963, having had a brilliant playing career with Derby and in particular Sheffield United, where he remains an absolute legend. He certainly shook things up at The Hawthorns and set about putting his mark on the club after some of the sparkle of Vic Buckingham's long reign had been lost. Although the managerial comings and goings that followed our 1950s highs weren't hectic by today's standards, there was probably a need for a longer period of building following the shortish reigns of Gordon Clark and Archie Macaulay. As their successor, Jimmy brought spells of brilliance, a host of memories and frequent brushes with controversy. His time in charge was never dull.

He never asked his players to do anything he couldn't or wouldn't do. He was always at the front in the stamina work during training, leading the way and making sure there were no shirkers. It was a bit different to the Macaulay days and a bit of a shock to the players at first because they found themselves having to run and run and run. He even had the corners taken off the pitch at the training ground at Spring Road, so it was a gradual bend and they didn't have to check their stride. The playing area was as big as Wembley and the excellent drainage meant it was a lovely surface. Well, it would be.....it wasn't used that often. I don't remember him working specifically on the defence (our goals against column probably underlined that), nor did there seem to be much specific concentration on the forwards. There was little pattern of play either because it was all running. Warm-ups comprised so many quarter-laps, so many half-laps and so many full laps. Then, once they were warmed up, they ran. One day, they went up to Clent Hills or Lickey Hills and were told to collect four different types of leaves. The players laughed at the idea but it was all about awareness and speed of eye. When they eventually saw a ball, they loved it. Maybe that's why they were so good with it. They were encouraged to treat it with respect and to measure a pass. If they couldn't keep it and find one of their colleagues, they couldn't wait to get it back. They really looked forward to matches…..it was 90 minutes with a ball.

At Spring Road, if a player went out to do some work with a ball on his own, he had to sign for one. It was Jimmy's way of giving him some responsibility, perhaps even without him knowing it. Today's players are much keener on taking the balls out than bringing them back. Often, the collecting is left to the youngsters or the coaching staff. Before training, the lads would have a lively game in the gym – anything from five-a-side to eight-a-side, so sometimes there wouldn't be much room. It would often be one-touch – they preferred it that way anyway because if they spent too much time on the ball, there was always someone close by to clatter them. I think we miss not having a gym at the new training ground now, excellent though it is. All Jimmy's players had to be honest and hard-working. He was like Gary Megson in demanding that type of character. He signed excellent pros like Johnny Kaye, Dougie Fraser, Jeff Astle, John Osborne, John Talbut and Eddie Colquhoun. He could spot a player and didn't make many mistakes in the transfer market. All those except Colquhoun, who was unlucky with injuries, were huge successes here. With the likes of Bobby Hope, Stan Jones, Bomber Brown, Don Howe, Graham Williams and Chippy Clark already at the club, we had a good team. I have very fond memories of that time and still have one of the striped shirts, which were so tight, and a pair of tiny light blue shorts – the ones used in training and very occasionally in away games. Kit was much less complicated then.

There was always a practice match in the week and Hagan invariably found an excuse for sending a player off for some minor misdemeanour – or just took him off by saying he wasn't doing things right. It was all so he could get on. And he usually stayed on. He could still play a bit and always fancied a game. I've heard Tony Brown say the lads all thought he was still terrific, although he was nearly 50. He was often the best player on the pitch apparently; his touch and passing were spot on. They were baffled why he didn't win more than his solitary England cap (other than wartime). After all that running, the players didn't spare him either when it came to a 50-50 ball. The fact he would do anything he asked them to, though – either in fitness work or on the training pitch – made it difficult for them to moan too much. And they appreciated the fact he was such a good player.

Even in the coldest weather, he would be out in his t-shirt and shorts, and matters came to a head in the winter of 1963-64 when he insisted the lads should do the same. The trainer Wilf Dixon was suddenly ordered to not put tracksuits out – an arrangement that meant I didn't have to spend long collecting the gear later for laundering. The players weren't even allowed to have underwear on and there was no sign whatsoever of gloves and woolly hats. He had us out with the boards once, shifting what seemed like two foot of snow and creating a path the players could run along, so no training was missed. He was quite fanatical. The players wanted to wear sweaters and tracksuit bottoms on the bitterest days. They were refused, so they went on strike and it was big news. We had the TV cameras at the training ground and the senior players like Don Howe, Graham Williams and Stan Jones told viewers of their complaints. The matter went on for several days and any number of transfer requests went in. Eventually, it was agreed they could warm up in sweaters and track bottoms as long as they came off for the actual session.

Jimmy seemed to have the knack of rubbing the players up the wrong way, yet still be able to extract plenty from them. Results were good even during this fractious period and a thrilling 4-4 home draw with Tottenham just after a compromise was found underlined that no serious damage had been done to the relationships. And the lads rallied to their gaffer's aid soon afterwards when he put his foot on the wrong pedal of his lovely Wolseley automatic and shot over the edge of the car park at Spring Road. He disappeared down a steep bank into the canal and by the time the players had rushed down there, he was sitting on the roof of the car. Fortunately, they had been able to pick up the stretcher from the treatment room and scramble down through the brambles and nettles to the towpath. He was still sufficiently in command to shout that he wanted four strong players to carry him to safety, naming Stan Jones and the goalkeepers Ray Potter and Tony Millington among them. With him plucked from danger, they had to walk a few hundred yards to get him up to the road by Spon Lane, where the ambulance could get to. Jimmy was in some discomfort with broken ribs but the story goes that he was still alert enough to notice that Millington was puffing and panting after responding to the emergency – and snapped at him: "You're not fit. Extra training for you!"

The directors had a moan at Hagan once about being too dictatorial and not communicative enough with the board and press. But he was totally different away from the club. The backroom staff were invited to a party at his home in Sutton Coldfield once and were told to wear something strange. I think I went in odd cufflinks or with a watchcase with no actual watch. Some were in odd socks and one or two ladies put on different ear-rings. Jimmy, much more subtly, had unbitten fingernails but had cut one of them very short. It was a strange ice-breaker looking someone over to try to spot what was different about them. Another game involved the men leaving the room, removing a sock and shoe and dangling a foot round the door while the women guessed who it belonged to. It was all very different to the Jimmy we knew during the week. I know it was a Saturday night because the games stopped while all the men went in one room to watch Match of the Day. Another game involved questions and sayings. If you got one wrong, you had a piece of soot dabbed on your forehead. Mine was a line of black spots. I was working with Jimmy daily but this get-together revealed a side of him that his work colleagues, let alone the fans, didn't know.

There was one aspect of training the lads enjoyed. They had to line up on the touchline facing the pitch and, in turn, kick the ball up in the air, so it bounced in the centre circle. The challenge was to then get to it before it bounced a second time. Failure to do so meant unpaid overtime for a few while they got it right. Kick the ball too high and it wouldn't reach; hit it too low and it would speed away from them. And it got harder, the more tired they became. Hopey and Bomber, for example, had the skill to master it. Stan Jones and one or two of the other defenders struggled. Players weren't allowed to go in until they had succeeded. Not that anyone would go in early and miss the fun anyway. They much preferred to sit around having a laugh at their mates' expense. I remember Jimmy being doubled up at the goings-on – he had obviously recovered from his broken ribs by then. He didn't have many lighter sides but that was one.

I mentioned earlier that Tony Brown lodged near where we lived.

Occasionally we'd meet for a game of pitch and putt in West Smethwick Park. Micky Fudge would come along as well, sometimes with a cricket bat and ball to make sure we got rid of all that youthful energy before bed-time. In September, 1963, when I was taking some fruit juice into the staff room, I saw the team sheet on the table and noticed that Bomber's name was on it. I shouldn't have told him and soon learned to be much more discreet but I was so excited for him that I relayed the news to him that he was making his debut in that weekend's game at Ipswich. He didn't believe me. I won't repeat the first word that came to his lips but the second one was 'off'. I had joined the club at about the same time as him and we became big mates as we knocked about together. He hasn't changed. He is such a nice guy and was the perfect pro. There aren't many you would point to and tell youngsters to model themselves on him but you would with him and you would with Kevin Phillips. Inevitably, Tony scored at Portman Road – and barely stopped scoring for us for almost 20 years. I can remember a picture, taken that afternoon in what was then our change strip of red shirts and white shorts, of our tiny forward line comprising Kenny Foggo, Bomber, Ronnie Fenton, Alec Jackson and Chippy Clark. We won 2-1.

I didn't travel to away games in those days, at least not with my job. I often went with my mates, though, and recall seeing Jock Wallace, who had the broadest accent of the many Scots we've had at the club, playing well in one of them at Bolton. Wilf Dixon, who was Harry Catterick's right-hand man at Everton when we beat them in the 1968 FA Cup final, was the trainer alongside Jimmy Hagan and we used to help him make sure nothing was forgotten before the team hit the road. Wilf would unload the kit at the other end. There was one wicker basket and a smaller one with the boots in, and a doctor's medical bag which the physio Fred Pedley would have put together. Even without motorways, there were very few overnight trips, so we would pack the skip on a Friday, then I or more often Harry Ashley would go in on a Saturday morning and see them off, just in case someone cried off overnight and you had to change the boots over. Harry didn't travel with the team either. They'd be gone about 9.30 for an average Lancashire trip to Manchester or Merseyside and I'd often travel with my mates Ray Law and Dave Tranmer either by car, train or coach. I'd go to a fair few. In the 1968 Cup run, for example, we went to Portsmouth and for the two trips to face Liverpool. I just used to pay at the turnstiles. It never occurred to me to ask at Albion for a ticket. I was still a fan. I even went with my mates to the 1967 League Cup final – after packing the skip with our all red change strip in, of course. There was no thought of me travelling with the team.

It was a huge adventure to see the M1 open for the first time. If I remember right, that was when I was on a coach going to Luton, possibly before I started at the club. It was a stretch of road we would get to know pretty well thanks to our success in the cups, especially, but I took in a few other prestige matches at Wembley in my younger years. Ray Law, who didn't work for Albion, had a car and I went with him to Cup finals. Tickets were always sent to the club and I remember buying one for him and seeing Tottenham, who had knocked us out in the fifth round, beat Burnley in 1962. Old Harry gave me his ticket to sell outside the ground after we had been made aware that they were fetching loads when Tottenham played Leicester the previous year. I failed miserably. Eventually, a lad at the turnstile gave me 2s 6d, which was less than face value. I couldn't bring myself to tell Harry I didn't even get its proper price. With that in mind, we went back in 1963 without tickets, thinking we would pick one up outside the stadium for next to nothing. Again we failed and sat outside until the last 20 minutes, although we still saw a couple of the goals as Manchester United, who included Johnny Giles, beat Leicester.

I was finding life less problematic at Spring Road, which was becoming an increasingly important part in Albion life. I tended to be based there while Harry stayed at The Hawthorns and I have fond memories of the lay-out. There were three dressing rooms plus a staff changing room (which doubled as the officials' room when matches were held there), boot room, drying room/kit room, tea room and kitchen. Upstairs were another tea room and kitchen, toilets, the treatment room (with a rehab area attached), a viewing room for parents to watch their youngsters, the manager's office, coach's office and a games room at the end, which catered for table tennis, pool, darts, chess and dominoes. We also had a telephone room with pay phones in. There was some tremendous fun up there and I recall Jeff Astle taking on Ray Matts of the Express & Star in a table tennis marathon that had quite a bit riding on it. All the lads were crowded round yelling as Jeff just kept getting the ball back from further and further away from the table. It was a place where the team bonded and camaraderie was built up.

The treatment room was brilliant, with its tables at one end and the physio area at the other. It also had a sun lamp which was popular with the more vain lads and the younger ones who were trying to get rid of their acne. Dick Sheppard was a good keeper but flash with it and had the habit of letting the ball go slightly past him before grabbing it. He used to spend ages grooming his hair and, of course, that was a magnet for the lads to want to mess with it after games. He would even go into the shower with a bucket on his head so he wouldn't disturb his hair. Dick was usually near the front of the sun lamp queue and had to run the gauntlet of mickey-taking once after reminding us what a slave he was to his appearance. He duly put the goggles on but exposed himself to those rays much longer than he should have done and was ribbed mercilessly by the lads because of his white bits – or Panda eyes as they became known. Many of the others were more inclined to catch a few rays if they knew we were going to be playing in all white. They reckoned it made them look like Real Madrid. Much later, Paul Mardon was another vain one. If he had a stitch above his eye, he would see it as a blow to his modelling career. He wasn't exactly the same as John Wile, John Kaye or Gareth McAuley for putting his head in. Red-haired Gerry Howshall, one of Dick's contemporaries, did his bit to keep the treatment room busy, though. I'd say he was the first of the hypochondriacs of my era. He wouldn't play unless he was absolutely 100 per cent.

The gym at Spring Road was where the lads would have fiercely competitive warm-up games or head tennis and where the weights room was located. That latter facility has been missed – it was never replaced after we looked for a new training ground in the 1980s. And the idea of having three dressing rooms was a good one because it was a rite of passage for players to get promoted from one to another. Apprentices kept the place neat and tidy and had to do some painting in the close season. The walls were a pale yellow. One of the Irish lads – it might well have been Ray 'Paddy' Treacy – once painted the floor grey and decided to do so by starting at the door. Did he think he could fly back, so there wouldn't be any footprints? Tony Brown and Asa Hartford were among the 1960s apprentices. Len Cantello came a little later, then Ally Robertson and, in the 1970s, the likes of Bryan Robson, John Trewick and Derek Statham. They all mucked in and did their share. I recall Ally helping me with the first team's training kit at Spring Road while he was still a teenager in the reserve or youth side. Bryan said in his autobiography how he once walked into the first team dressing room to collect some kit and Yorky Kaye bellowed at him: "You, out! Knock next time when you want to come in." His punishment for stepping out of line was to have to dance with a mop in the middle of the dressing room in front of the lads. It was a way of learning respect.

Cleaning boots and sweeping the floors used to be part of the youngsters' chores. These guys, huge Albion favourites all of them, had to go through that apprenticeship. They weren't pampered like lads are these days. 'Chop-chop, busy-busy' was one of my favourite sayings to get them moving in the mornings – I used it at home as well with the girls. And there was nothing like the training gear that's available in the dressing room now. It was t-shirt, sweater, shorts and socks only. My values come from their era. It was a different era and I'd say a better one. Apprentices didn't get away with much, even star boys like Pop Robson and Derek Statham. If they didn't do their jobs properly, they did them again and I was known to give them a sneaky cleaning test by creating some extra mess where they might not expect me to look. I've seen a group of lads jump on a bus into West Brom thinking they were finished and I drove the minibus in, met them and brought them straight back to tidy something up. I've also been known to stop the minibus and make someone pick up litter that has been thrown from the window. If it were up to me, I would send first-year apprentices out to smaller clubs to open their eyes. It's not their fault but if Albion are their first club, this is all they know. They have no sense of perspective. About 20 years ago, we despatched some lads to Scarborough and Scunthorpe for ten days just for the experience and they were back after a couple of nights. They couldn't hack having to train in socks with holes in. It made them appreciate more what they had with us.

There were drawbacks to what we used to have. The fact there was only one grass pitch at Spring Road didn't help. There was a shale all-weather one as well but then the M5 was built and the noise down by the artificial surface was too much. There was concern as well at the pollution. Despite these problems, I have such happy memories of the place. It was where some exhilarating Albion sides were groomed – cup-winning teams with great characters and entertainers. And it was where some astute minds started to turn from playing to coaching. John Jarman took over from Wilf Dixon and persuaded several of our senior players, like Ronnie Fenton, Don Howe, Graham Williams and maybe Bobby Robson, to take their badges. John's peculiarity during a game was turning the medical bucket upside down to let the players know there were five minutes left. I suppose it was so you didn't have to shout and let the opposition know as well.

I missed out on knowing Maurice Setters, who is reputed to have kicked all the balls into the Atlantic on the way to America in 1959 so the players didn't have to do any training while on board ship. Davey Burnside went for a much softer touch and needed only one ball to enthral a packed Hawthorns with his famous juggling act at half-time in the floodlight-opening friendly against the Russian Red Army. Here's a secret, though: they took a bit of air out of the ball so it was less lively and came down softer but he still performed wonders to make sure he didn't let it hit the ground once. David was at the club in my early months and Barry Hughes, one of his contemporaries, was one I'd like to have got to know better. He didn't make the first team but players apparently used to go into training earlier to be entertained by him, with his jokes and stories. He went later to Holland, where he had a good career in coaching, then to Belgium, where he married a singer and had his own TV show. Alec Jackson was another who kept us with smiles on our faces. In the close season, he would take on Harry Ashley at Sandwell Park or Dartmouth. Selwyn Vale would caddy for one and me for the other.

Above all, we were kept happy by what we saw on the pitch because they were high-scoring days, more often than not spent in the top half of the First Division. I was still proud to be working for the club I loved and things moved on for me during Jimmy Hagan's reign. Harry and Selwyn both left and I found myself in sole charge of running the kit side of the operation as well as, on occasions, helping with other general maintenance, especially forking the pitch and putting top soil on. It was now my job – and no-one else's – to put those famous striped shirts on the players' backs.

Chapter Four

Some Silverware To Savour

Look at those stirring Albion pictures of the 1960s and one thing stands out. Our kit wasn't supplied by a major company, such as Umbro, Adidas or Bukta. There are no logos. Instead, we dealt with a sports shop in West Bromwich called Dickens, who were based not far from the billiard hall and near where the Three Degrees statue will be located. The proprietor kept two spare sets in case we had a fire at the ground or the laundry and lost everything. He still had this kit many years later and asked if we wanted it because it was no use to him. There were short-sleeved and long-sleeved shirts, a set of shorts designed by Matt Busby and those distinctive socks with the two navy hoops just above the ankle. There's no sponsor name – and the red numbers were clearly visible because they were in a white box on the players' backs. I loved it. Later, we dealt with Ron Goodman of Goodman Sports from Southgate, London, who supplied several clubs and the home countries. Toomers of Southampton were another in between the two, probably instigated by Stuart Williams, who settled down that way as a Southampton player before coming back as our assistant manager.

The kit might have appeared more basic but there were still innovations. When we had a spate of ankle injuries once, probably because of all the pounding of the running track, Jimmy Hagan had a Winit boot made for us. They were called the WBA Specials and offered more support as they came higher up the ankle. The toe caps were rock-hard in comparison with the soft leather of the uppers and the players used to hammer them to make them more pliable. They reminded me of the old McGregor boots, which the older generation might recall, and I would have thought it was best to have left them as they were. No opponent in his right mind would fancy getting caught by them when going in for a tackle with Dougie Fraser, Yorky Kaye or Graham Williams. They used to like that particular footwear for when they thought there was someone they owed one to. "One challenge from you and we won't see him again in the game," I used to tell them. Players didn't have to wear shin pads then but they do now. Chippy Clark was too brave for his own good and used to have his socks rolled right down.

There were other notable differences. There was more of an innocence about the game then and players were keen to top up their earnings through other bits of work. There were no millionaire lifestyles, that's for sure, nor an endless supply of jobs in the media. Kenny Stephens, who could be a world-beater in a practice match but couldn't do it regularly on a match day, worked in a hospital as a porter in the summer and pulled pints at night at The Talbot on Smethwick High Street. Dick Krzywicki, one of Kenny's rivals for the right-wing position in the 1968 Cup run, used to work in Dartmouth Garage and our young centre-half, Ron Potter, was training to be a barber in Wolverhampton. He couldn't drive, so I used to take him and he would pay me back by cutting my hair for nothing. The boss there would finish it off. They wanted me to be a model because I had such thick hair and they could do any style on it. I politely declined. Much more recently, Ron came to our hotel when we were preparing for an away game. He was involved in the auction business by then and Frank Burrows, who knew him from Swindon, had stayed in touch with him. They go out socially. I left a message for Ron once and said I could do with a haircut.

I always had my eye out for earning a bit on the side. Dennis Clarke used to bring lengths of material from the mills as samples and I would act as an agent by selling them to the players. I still have enough camel for a nice coat. That wasn't all. For a while, after the couple who supplied the catering bars round the ground got fed up, I did the cheese butties as well. I was with Carol by then and we spent Friday nights doing 200-300 cobs. I think we could have ended up doing them for Villa and Manchester City as well if we'd had the time and inclination. Another sideline was delivering the Albion Pools all round Smethwick. I'd collect the envelopes on a Monday lunchtime after picking up Carol and sort out a route for pushing them through doors later. To make sure I was well attired for my additional tasks, I'd buy up vouchers the club gave us for a gents' outfitters in West Brom. A few of the lads weren't bothered about going clothes shopping, so I'd pay them half what their vouchers were worth and treat myself to a few shirts.

A colourful character on the scene in the 1960s was Ernie Hart, who ran a café near the Villa ground and would get anything for the lads. He'd come up with tickets for big games and used to turn up at Spring Road with his boot full of all sorts of stuff off lorry drivers who stopped by for a cuppa. I bought some car covers and blankets off him, Bobby Hope purchased a handbag for his wife, and Campbell Crawford opted for some M & S shirts, all at the right price, of course. They didn't fit, so Ernie told him to take them to the store and change them for some that did. Some of the players – Graham Williams, John Kaye and Doug Fraser, if my memory serves me correctly – had carpets off him but he rang them in a panic and told them to rip them up. Apparently they were so 'hot' that they were in danger of burning their feet and the police were on to the source of it. Ernie had the gift of the gab. He used to call himself the Lord Mayor of Witton when he rang up to ask for match tickets and car parking passes, and the office girls fell for it every time. They made it their duty to make sure he could leave his latest luxury vehicle in safety.

The social scene around the club was good. We were once told we'd be welcome at a doctor's daughter's 21st birthday party in Harborne. The invitation was left on the table of the dressing room and was aimed more at the younger, single players. I thought it had been ignored, so I asked my mates if they fancied going. We turned up and said: "We've come on behalf of the players because they have had an away match" but they were already there and legged it in case Jimmy Hagan was at the door with us. Slowly, they started to reappear when they realised he wasn't and we all went on to the Cedar Club in Birmingham. Dick Sheppard, Graham Lovett, Micky Fudge and Dick Krzywicki were the likely candidates. Graham was great fun but a nightmare behind the wheel of a car. How he passed his test, I don't know. He was absolutely hopeless, yet the lads would still pile in his car after training (more than should have been in there probably) and go up to West Brom High Street for their lunch. It's so sad that he had two serious road accidents which left him with bad spinal and neck injuries that meant he came back with metal pins. We joked that we would have to carry an oil can and spanner in the skip so he didn't come apart in a game. What a good player he was! He was so hard to knock off the ball because of his strength and desperately unlucky not to fulfil his potential. I was always reminded of him much later when I watched Roy Keane.

I took chances of my own on the road on occasions, although the breathalyser laws were nothing like they are now. All the drinks at one Christmas party at the Ambassador's Club in Edgbaston were free, so I got stuck into the Sam Brown's until it ran out. I then went on to Guinness and finally hit the Newcastle Brown. I had to go into West Brom afterwards to drop off a young player and his girlfriend before going home to Smethwick and my passengers, including Carol, came in very useful en route. They had to tell me whether the traffic lights were on green. Smethwick Cricket Club at Broomfield Park was our regular drinking hole. I wasn't a cricketer but my mate Ray was and he would probably know whether we are still banned from the West Bromwich Football League. He was a bit older than me but became involved as sponge man for the Littlemoor Boys' Sunday team who I played for. We were always in debt and used to get fines for not fulfilling fixtures, failing to provide linesmen and inadequate upkeep of the pitch. We later moved to Hadley Stadium and just wanted to play. We couldn't be bothered with all the administration that came with running a club. If someone was sent off and suspended, we'd just play him under another name. The secretary went to the meetings to face the music and eventually the club and all connected with it were given bans until the money was paid. It never was, so I take it I and we are still banned. There was one consolation, though. When I had left school and was working at Albion, we had the best kit in the league – blue and white stripes, of course.

I was still playing when I met Carol and she used to come to the dances we held to try to bail ourselves out with some much-needed funds. I was getting to the age when she was taking over as a priority, so it wasn't such a blow not to be playing. The team dissolved but we had some good fun before going our separate ways. It was an interesting mix, including Papa, who had an ice cream round, and Derek and Ron – that's the Lowe brothers, not Kevan and Allen. I must have been a better player than I was an administrator because I turned out twice for Albion, first at Mansfield in the Midland Intermediate League when we also had first-team and reserve matches on the same Saturday. I played at left-back and was a bit nervous but Jim Holton and Gordon Nisbet were in the side and it was great to play at a proper stadium. There was only one sub in those days and I suppose I was flattered when the switch was made and someone else was taken off. I still have the cutting out of the Evening Mail. The following weekend, when I wasn't included, I knocked on the manager's door and, tongue-in-cheek, asked why I had been left out. I played once the following year as well and again it was Mansfield, this time at Spring Road. They must have thought I was a regular. Not that Alistair Robertson would have appreciated it if I had been. He played in that home game.

We were so well stocked with quality players that my services were never going to be required very often. In 1965-66, we finished sixth in the First Division and our haul of 91 League goals was loads more than any other side. We also won the League Cup in our first season of entering, with the Walsall tie at The Hawthorns watched by more than 41,000 and producing a great atmosphere. Coventry at home was another wonderful night. We thrashed them 6-1 and big Jeff scored a hat-trick. We also defeated Villa 3-1 and Leeds 4-2 away. We were a very fit, strong-running team but played outstanding football as well. After we had overcome Third Division Peterborough over two games in the semi-final, this time with Bomber hitting a hat-trick, I went to the home and away legs of the final against West Ham. At Upton Park, we played five at the back for the first time, with young Danny Campbell making his debut as one of the central defenders and Graham Williams in the no 6 shirt after missing much of the season through injury. It was obviously aimed at stopping West Ham but didn't really work because we came away losing 2-1. The second leg was an outstanding night, though; one people still talk of with great fondness all these decades on. We were brilliant and won 4-1 to take the cup on a 5-3 aggregate. To help the celebrations along, Paddy Ryan underlined his Irish roots by bringing in a few crates of Export Guinness, which was hard to get hold of at the time. He knew everyone and had no such problems. I kept a bottle and took it along as an auction prize when we had a reunion of the team in 2006. It seemed fitting that someone paid £40 for it – a pound for every year of its life.

The victory meant we were in Europe for the first time but 1966-67 was a difficult season. We lost seven of the first ten games in the League despite scoring 23 goals. The neutrals loved watching us because we conceded just as many. Clive Clark showed over and over again what a good winger he was. He used to get battered by full-backs but kept coming back for more and was our top scorer that year by a distance. We were a free-flowing, attacking team, who were very easy on the eye, and Chippy netted in all seven of the games we played in another great League Cup run. Ironically, it was that competition that did for Jimmy Hagan. Thanks to another sequence of high-scoring wins, including a semi-final thrashing of West Ham, we were on the brink of retaining the cup when we led QPR, from the Third Division, 2-0 at half-time in the final. But we contrived to lose 3-2 at a time when we were also in a relegation battle.

I recall going with my mates to a club in Birmingham to drown our sorrows after we had suffered at Rodney Marsh's feet in the competition's first Wembley final. We eventually won eight of the last ten games – and scored even more heavily than at the start of the season – to stay up with plenty to spare as the Villa went down with Blackpool. But that run wasn't enough to save Jim, whose hard-line ways had led to a number of further transfer requests from leading players in the autumn. Some of the squad may have been happy to see the back of him but I was sorry when his time came to an end. More often than not, we were entertained by some cracking matches on a Saturday and I was even more grateful to think I'd then be working with the same players on a Monday.

Chapter Five

A Memorable Wembley Date

Alan Ashman was so different to Jimmy Hagan and the players immediately took to him. They relished his relaxed attitude and found it very refreshing after Jimmy's Sergeant Major ways. Good foundations were in place and there was no doubt the squad knew what peak fitness was all about. But Alan was softer-natured and the lads responded to that. The shackles came off and he was able to get the best out of the many good players Jimmy had signed, like Doug Fraser, Jeff Astle and the three Johns – Kaye, Osborne and Talbut. With Tony Brown, Bobby Hope, Clive Clark and skipper Graham Williams around as well, it's no wonder we had some great times. Alan wasn't well known around the Midlands when he was appointed in the summer of 1967. At that time, I don't think we had ever played Carlisle (the club he came down to us from) and people in the game, other than at the very top, didn't have anything like the profile they would do today. He could probably have walked down West Bromwich High Street unrecognised because he had even had a stint working as a chicken farmer since the end of his playing days. A year after his appointment, there was barely a yard of space on that High Street as the team came back on a rainy Sunday afternoon displaying the FA Cup.

Albert McPherson was one of the coaches Alan inherited. He had been part of Jimmy Hagan's backroom team and had the difficult job of organising the kit on the long tour of South America in 1966. I got on well with him. He's a lovely guy. He never swore or said anything worse than 'flippin this' and 'floppin that,' unlike some managers I can name. I'm amazed more don't get sent from the dug-out. The former Wolves inside-forward Jimmy Dunn was there waiting for Alan, too, but Stuart Williams was brought back to the club in 1967 as Alan's assistant and the atmosphere at Spring Road was brilliant.

The players would be up in the games room long after training. Alan recognised the need for good camaraderie and was keen to see them enjoying each others' company over games of table tennis, pool, billiards, darts or whatever. Big Jeff was usually at the centre of it. At table tennis at least, he wasn't the best player by any means and I recall certain opponents having to give him a ten-point start. But he had the happy knack of drawing his team-mates around him by being such great fun. Needless to say, a bit of money used to change hands in betting on the outcome of matches.

Alan, a quietly spoken Yorkshireman who had spent most of his playing career as a prolific scorer for Carlisle, encouraged the lads to live near each other in Gillity Village between Walsall and Great Barr. Maybe at different times, Tony Brown and John Kaye lived two doors away (on opposite sides) from Alan himself and other nearby residents were John Talbut and, some time later, Ally Robertson and the goalkeeper Graham Smith. Alan thought sensible socialising between them and their wives was a good thing. Perhaps it was also so he could keep an eye on them. Most of them liked a pint but, as I recall, didn't indulge to excess. They were a good group and bonded famously. The whole squad got on well, with no shortage of pranks. John Osborne used to go out early with the ball for some shooting-in and became a victim of the practical jokers one day. While he was out, some of the others cut the legs off his trousers because they thought they were so shabby. They hung them up to make them look as though they were intact. The laugh was on him but they made amends by having a whip-round and putting enough in his pocket for him to buy a replacement pair. He joked that he was going to come in the next day in another old pair that needed replacing.

The lads didn't see much of Ossie on a Friday. He never seemed to be fit that day. He was always going to pull out of a match; either he had a cold, or backache, or knee problems. Then there was that issue with his 'bionic' knuckle that opened up a whole load of fresh doubts. "See how you are in the morning" was the common phrase. And, almost invariably, he would pass himself fit, pull those shorts up tight and perform well. Ossie was fitted with a plastic knuckle and had to adapt his gloves by opening up the seams and then stitching them back together with one double-size finger space because his joint swelled. He had to keep away from anything hot to avoid the risk of melting. That handicap must just have added to his legendary nervousness. The players often looked round for him just before they went down the tunnel at five to three because he had disappeared to the loo for a cigarette. At other times, he would be puffing on a pipe. Not that he was alone in smoking.

The likes of John Kaye, Big T and Chippy Clark enjoyed lighting up in the dressing room after a game because it wasn't frowned on then. And Ally Brown and Willie Johnston of the 1970s lads were known to disappear for a smoke to ease their nerves before a game. Afterwards, players would have a cigarette or beer in the bath and talk about the match. Now, the big baths have gone for health reasons. An ice bath might be taken by some but the usual routine is: Shower, dress, meet the family, off. The smoking ban has to be good but something has been lost. An opportunity for cultivating some team spirit has gone. Ossie had other characteristics. He liked bird watching and was the star of the Albion line-up, also including Alan Ashman, Doug Fraser and motocross star Jeff Smith, who won BBC TV's Quiz Ball competition in 1968. The impressive trophy is still on display in one of the cabinets at the ground.

Yorky Kaye was one of my heroes. He was down-to-earth and gave you all he had, whether it was as a forward or, later on, a defender. I love that photo of him with the sticky tape over his eye the night he was badly cut and then stitched up when we beat Liverpool in a quarter-final second replay on the way to winning the FA Cup in Alan's first season. That well-deserved cigarette is there, too. What can I say about big Jeff? He was the life and soul of the place. My dad had a greyhound called Reska running for a time and Jeff loved going to the dogs with me once a week or so. He would often report to The Hawthorns, supposedly to watch a reserve game, and then slope off to Perry Barr or Wolverhampton and have a bet. I'd tell him if the dog was in good form and the trainer expected him to win. If it did come home first, he'd give me a ten bob note out of his winnings and tell me not to let on to his wife that he'd had a bit of luck. He would just go and buy an item of furniture so he couldn't give it back to the bookie next time. If he lost, he'd make a big song and dance when he had a decent audience and shout at my dad: "There's the owner….there's the guy who has lost you all your money."

One of Jeff's later attacking partners, Colin Suggett, was another who loved a flutter. His passion for racing pigeons and going to the greyhounds ensured we always had good chit-chat. I used to drive Jeff to some meetings before he had a licence and we had great fun. We were about the same age and he was a gentleman who just loved his working-class pleasures like a game of dominoes in the pub. We got on well and had good banter. He was cursed later on by knee troubles and had problems once with his appendix. What people round the club suspected was that he had two other lesser-known conditions – Curtisitis and McGrathitis. As much as he loved playing and scoring against the likes of Manchester United and West Ham, because he always terrorised them in the air, he used to get ribbed for barely leaving the centre circle when he faced Coventry's George Curtis and Southampton's John McGrath. They seemed to have a hold on him at times.

Others have beaten me to telling the story of how he used to do his routine when the referee came into the dressing room to make sure there were no sharp edges on the players' studs. Another famous story is of the day Alan Ashman arrived ready to do his team talk for a game and Jeff asked him to wait while the players finished watching a race on TV. Years before, there would have been a different type of pre-match entertainment as relaxation. Chess was played in the dressing room in my first season or two – possibly as a result of Don Howe's interest – and it's where I learned to play. Cricket was the choice of Ronnie Allen, Dave Burnside and Bobby Robson. They loved the game. There wasn't room for hitting out but the idea was for the batsman just to frustrate the bowler, who had to rely on under-arm spinners with the litter bins as the wicket, with everyone crowded round waiting for a catch.

Things didn't immediately click under Alan Ashman's management, for Jeff Astle or anyone else. We started his first season quite poorly and lost at Reading – then of the Third Division – in our first game in the League Cup. But signs of improvement came. Whereas Jimmy Hagan's philosophy seemed to revolve around just attacking, perhaps because he had been a brilliant forward himself, Alan's preparations were a bit more all-round. We gradually gained the reputation of being a side who were hard to beat. Jimmy hadn't really bothered with signing defenders until near the end of his reign, then he brought in John Talbut, Eddie Colquhoun and Ossie in quick succession, although Eddie was to break his ankle in an Easter game at Newcastle at a time when he may well have gone on to play in the FA Cup final. I suppose Alan had the benefit of Big T and Ossie settling in and it was Eddie's misfortune that led to Yorky Kaye being converted successfully from a fearless forward to a lion-hearted central defender.

Even so, we had that narrow escape in the third round of the Cup at Colchester (another team from Division Three) before going through easily when the replay attracted a big crowd of nearly 40,000. We also had the curiosity, by today's standards, of us playing that tie at The Hawthorns in our change strip of all red. There was a time when both teams had to change in the Cup in the event of a clash, although both ourselves and Southampton used our regular kit at home when the fourth-round meeting also went to a replay. By then, we had adopted all white as our lucky change kit and the photos show we wore it when we won in a thriller at The Dell – a game which illustrated another way in which things were different then. When Ossie went off injured, Graham Williams took over in goal and was swamped by the keeper jersey, which came down over his fingers. Clearly, there was no thought about carrying a spare green top in the skip for emergencies. White was our colour again when we won in the fifth round at Portsmouth and was the preferred option by now, in the Cup at least. When we drew at home to Liverpool in the quarter-final, there was no thought of packing the blue and white stripes for Anfield. We wore white there as well and also when we squeezed through a thrilling second replay at Maine Road, which I look back on as one of the great nights of the Ashman era. It was such a courageous performance to get through against the odds. We even lost the toss to have choice of venue for the third match against Bill Shankly's warm favourites. We would have chosen Villa Park but their correct call meant we had to head back up to Lancashire, where the balance of support was in their favour. Those three games against Liverpool were titanic, all the more so as both sides knew a game against Second Division Birmingham awaited them in the semi-final. That local derby at Villa Park was all about us keeping our nerve really. It was a very tense occasion and Blues played well despite their 2-0 defeat, so the relief at getting to Wembley was huge.

The replacement of all red with all white (although we still used red for some away League games) wasn't the only change to our routine. As Jimmy Hagan had done before a League game at Manchester City the season before, Alan started to use Southport as a base for the squad before the matches in the latter stages of the Cup run. The team spirit became even better on those trips. Getting all the players pulling together was something Alan was very good at. Some latitude was given and I wondered whether the lads might become too comfortable with him in the long run and perhaps take advantage. But you do what's right at the time to get good results and it worked for us. We were more than decent in the League as that season wore on – and finished eighth in the table – but we were red-hot in the FA Cup run, as we had been in the League Cup for the previous couple of years.

Raw egg, sherry and jelly, beaten up and downed in one, was one of the strange rituals for the lads in the 1960s. All the players had one, so did I, and my dad followed suit when he was feeling low. Anything for a free drink. But I needed a little something extra after an over-indulgence that showed Alan's tolerant side. I drank more than I should have done at a party and remember being sat on a table up against a nice warm boiler and basically being hung over for three days. I told the players to help themselves to their kit. Fortunately, Alan turned a blind eye. He was so easy-going. Even more fortunately, I knew where to go for a remedy. I had been an occasional visitor to Bannister and Thatcher's chemist on West Bromwich High Street to buy various medication and dressings for the players and gradually befriended a young lady who worked there. Having had my eye caught by her nice smile and friendly face, I eventually plucked up the courage to ask her out and could hardly go wrong with our first date. It was to the FA Cup final.

Carol Ewen, as she then was, leaned towards her home-town team Walsall rather than Albion, partly because her dad was a Saddlers supporter. So she probably had only a passing interest in the run that captivated me. Not that it was only the Cup games that brought out the best in the side. If there's one match I look back on from that time with special fondness, other than the big ties, it's Albion 6 United 3. What a night! I'll say it again: What a night! The official attendance was just under 46,000 but many got in for free when a gate was broken down. Thousands of others were locked out. We had beaten Blues in a tough semi-final only two days before and were without John Kaye and Clive Clark through injury against United. But the lads somehow found it in themselves to put the reigning League champions (a side who were pushing for another title and were just about to win the European Cup) to the sword. We led 6-1 at one point as big Jeff scored three times to go past the 30-goal mark for the season. We didn't even need our lucky white kit that night. The traditional one did the job very nicely.

Things just kept rolling and it was a great time. Our League finish of eighth was our best since 1960 and Jeff managed another hat-trick – against West Ham under the magical Hawthorns lights – as Alan kept the players' minds on the First Division programme as best he could. With Everton as our Wembley opponents, it was obvious another colour change was required. Like in the semi-final against Blues, both teams went for their second strip, with Everton wearing the amber and blue they had sported when winning 6-2 at our place in the League a few weeks earlier. We were in white, of course, but unusually in red socks rather than white ones. I've been asked why that was and have put the same question to the lads but still have no idea. The dilemma did throw up one of the more memorable headlines a couple of years ago, though, when the excellent Backpass magazine did a big feature on us and used the heading 'Bostin Red Socks' on one of the pieces.

I think we got a cash bonus when we won the Cup but not a lot. It didn't seem to matter. It was just a tremendous day for us all, even if it wasn't the most memorable final for the country at large. I thought the lads looked smart in their specially made new white tracksuits, although Graham Williams reckons they weren't run off with Wembley in mind. They had already been done apparently in readiness for the tour of East Africa the lads went on a couple of days after beating Everton. The final was particularly special for me with going out with Carol for the first time – and it obviously wasn't only the team who impressed her. I must have done something right as well. We had a meal on the train going down there from my local station Rolfe Street and decided against having a meal and champagne on the train back in favour of staying over in London in the company of my friends Stuart, John, Roy and Derek. That might not have been my best decision.

For a start, Carol might have been a little happier if she had had a roof over her head. We were going to kip down at an aunt's in Wimbledon but decided that the 10pm curfew imposed on us was not really what we wanted when we were celebrating winning the FA Cup. So we had a meal in an Angus Steakhouse and a few drinks – followed by a few more – before finding ourselves in St James's Park in the early hours instead of a warm abode in South London. We took a deckchair each and one of us even made a shelter out of some spare ones but the police didn't like our handiwork. They moved us on, although our worst crime was just being merry. It was a cold night, so we warmed up with a full English breakfast before catching the milk train back very early on the Sunday. I picked up my car, took Carol back to Walsall, where she still lived, snatched some much-needed sleep and failed to make the parade when the team arrived back with the Cup. I missed the bloody lot! I struggled to live it down over the years, especially with some of the office staff, who were with us for the main part of a great weekend before sorting themselves out properly for the return journey.

Margaret Limbrick, then Margaret Round, was the manager's secretary at Albion for nearly ten years and she and her partner John (later her husband) looked after Alan and Beryl Ashman's children David and Deborah for the weekend. They stayed over at a hotel in Walsall on the Friday and Saturday nights and went to the match in between. She tells me how surprised she was in being able to walk past security up the tunnel at Wembley and take the two kids into the dressing room to see their dad just before the game, when the players were all changed and virtually ready to go out. We've stayed in contact with Margaret over the years and she came back to work at the club for a while after having her family. Janet Willetts (later Janet Thompson) was another of the girls in the office in 1968 and went on the train with her friend. Come to think of it, I may still owe Albion for Carol's ticket.......

Chapter Six

Chasing More Cup Glory

On the Monday after the final, while the team were preparing to go off on what proved to be a stormy tour to East Africa, I was lucky to be given Jeff Astle's change shirt. I also got the blank (unnumbered) one. As kit-man, I was first in line for such pickings. There wasn't anything like the same interest in memorabilia then, although the players liked their own souvenirs of a big day. The general rule, though, was that if nobody else put in a claim for items, I had them. It was one of the perks of the job. I found that out to my good fortune over and over again down the decades and made a nice sum when I sold Jeff's spare shirt – with the permission of his widow Laraine – not long ago. Not that he ever shut up about what he did for me. In 1971, when we moved into our first house, he was still telling me that he had bought it with all the goals he had scored and the bits of bonus money that had gone into my account as a result. I wasn't going to just take that. I went back at him by saying that if he had scored more, we could have had a detached instead of a semi.

We had a decent run in the European Cup Winners Cup the following season, better than we had managed a couple of years earlier in the Inter Cities Fairs Cup anyway. We made it to the quarter-final before losing on a bitterly cold night at The Hawthorns against Dunfermline – the first time I ever saw outfield players in gloves. Our lads were real men and not easily put off by a bit of mud and rain but this tie was played in a blast from Siberia and several of them went for an accessory that has become commonplace in recent years. By contrast, the sun shone when we took on Leicester in the FA Cup semi-final at Hillsborough towards the end of the same season. We were convinced we were going back to Wembley, especially as Leicester were on their way to getting relegated. We were still in the habit of packing that all white kit more than the stripes for away ties and both Fulham and Chelsea also changed colours when there was a clash for our victories down there in the fourth and sixth rounds. All white didn't seem quite so lucky, though, nor did Southport as a place to prepare for Cup games, after Ossie had been beaten late on by Allan Clarke's shot with the prospect of another Albion v Everton final looming. In the end, it was Leicester and Manchester City who got there.

We were nevertheless still a team to fear in knockout football. Although we flopped for a change in the FA Cup despite a memorable goal from Tony Brown at Sheffield Wednesday, we did make it back to Wembley in 1969-70. This time it was in the final of the League Cup in which we faced a Manchester City team containing Arthur Mann and Joe Corrigan. They were both lovely men and worked for us decades later, Arthur after being brought here by Alan Buckley as his no 2 and Joe when recruited by Bryan Robson as goalkeeper coach. The pitch for that final was the worst I'd ever seen at Wembley, surrounded by snow and covered in straw after a heavy downfall in the week and the staging of the Horse of the Year show not long before. There was the extra disappointment for us of losing in what was our third final appearance in the competition in only five years – and that after Jeff had headed us into an early lead. Look at the pictures. It must have been quite a job getting our whites white again after that afternoon in the mud.

There were changes on the field after the settled side of the mid and later 1960s. Graham Williams was coming towards the end of his career and had been replaced as skipper by Dougie Fraser while Alan Ashman made what was then quite a serious move in the transfer market by splashing out in the same summer on Colin Suggett, Danny Hegan, Allan Glover and Jimmy Cumbes. The purchases were only partly successful. Colin was a good player who had a decent scoring record here over a few years and Jim showed what a competent keeper he was before going on to better things elsewhere. The other two weren't a great success, although the presence of Danny, who was a Northern Ireland international, had a useful spin-off. On a Wednesday, the squad would sometimes give up their day off and go in to play a match between the English and the Celts (the Scots, Welsh and Irish) at Spring Road. If there was an imbalance, lads would be asked if they had ever been on holiday to Rhyl or Ben Nevis, or had grandparents from across the border. If they had, they would be switched. The staff would be banned unless they were prepared to play. Albert McPherson and Stuart Williams would join in but many others would take the more sensible option and stay out of the way. John Osborne and Jim Cumbes would both play outfield and it was fiercely competitive with the tackles flying in – all because the winners would have all the orange juice to themselves and the chance to gloat. The losers drank water. They would be sworn enemies on the pitch and then, the moment the games ended, they would be great mates again, exchanging banter in the bath.

It was at the end of that summer of big signings, 1969, that Gordon Nisbet made headlines. Ossie must have been injured on the opening day at Southampton because Gordon took over from him after lining up as a keeper in the youth and reserve sides. With him in goal, we were beaten 3-1 at Coventry and he went on to have a long career as a right-back, even playing for England under-23s. It's not rare for a player to change his position, particularly when they are young, but it's extremely unusual for anyone to go from being a goalkeeper to an outfield player. And we briefly then saw the reverse happen with Gordon. In the mid-1970s, Ossie was hurt in the build-up to us conceding a penalty in a Second Division match at Sunderland, so Gordon took the red keeper's shirt off him and went in goal while treatment was administered behind the goal. He didn't get within two yards of the penalty, which bounced back off the post before the rebound was whacked into the crowd. It was still 0-0, so Ossie went back in goal after partially recovering and after the lads had finished congratulating themselves on surviving the penalty. The only trouble was that we then conceded three goals in quick succession. With the battle lost, we accepted the inevitable and Gordon went in for the rest of the game. That bizarre sequence of events, all captured on Match of the Day and by the commentary of John Motson, was something else I never saw again.

Mind you, with Barry Davies at the microphone for a follow-up Saturday night appearance on BBC, there was uproar on another of our trips. It was near the end of 1970-71 and the day we won sensationally at Leeds. No-one would bat an eyelid now but the interpretation of the rules was different then. Tony Brown was waved on as Colin Suggett jogged back from an offside position and Bomber's cross was slotted in by Big Jeff, who may also have been offside. You can see from the TV footage how hostile it was, with Don Revie and his players blaming the officials for a decision that in hindsight cost them the title to Arsenal. I remember the lads saying we were brilliant that day and deserved to win but I know from personal experience that Elland Road can be a daunting place. There was one set of toilets that served both sides and it was well-known that if one of your players popped in before kick-off to spend a penny, he would soon be followed in by a couple of their hard cases. It was seen as an act of intimidation, if only verbal, but it was to no avail that day.

Unfortunately, with or without those points, and the one we took off Arsenal at The Hawthorns the following week, we could make little impact in the League. We had gone something like 17 months without winning away in the First Division until we beat Leeds and we finished in the bottom six. We didn't even have the excuse that we had been distracted by a good cup run. We went out fairly early in both competitions that season. The chairman Jim Gaunt had said he longed for us to challenge to win the title and fired Alan in the summer of 1971. I was sorry to see him go because he was a lovely man who the players responded to. That's why we won the FA Cup three years earlier. But you only respond for so long.

I have one other thing to be grateful to Alan for. It was he who gave me my Albion debut in the Midland Intermediate League at Mansfield. It was on the day of the FA Cup semi-final against Leicester and we all went on to Hillsborough after playing at Field Mill on the Saturday morning. That appearance wasn't my only involvement with the back-up teams. During Alan's four years in charge, I would sometimes have to stay and see to the kit for the reserves. There were 3,000 there sometimes because the games were played on Saturday afternoons and, every 15 minutes and at the end, the first-team score was put up on the scoreboard in the Woodman Corner of the ground. The blokes operating it used to wind the crowd up. You would see them carrying a big number across and there would be gasps from the spectators, who wondered whether the senior side had run riot or caved in. Then the pranksters would change it to a nought when they actually dropped it in place. Imagine the fun they must have had relaying back the events of that controversial afternoon at Leeds. Would our fans back at The Hawthorns have believed we could break our long away duck by winning so well at the home of the title challengers?

Alan died in 2002 and my ghost writer informs me that the headstone at Streetly Crematorium for his wife Beryl and him has 'AET 1-0' as its bottom line. Need I say more? FA Cup glory underlined that he helped give us some memorable times and I suppose I wish I had been as involved with the first team then, in terms of travelling with them, as I was to become very shortly. It would certainly have provided another chapter or two for this book. But I didn't have to rely on second-hand accounts of first-team away games for much longer. Thanks partly to us, Arsenal won the double in the May of 1971 and, with Don Howe's stock sky-high as he was credited with being the brains behind the operation, he was named as Alan's successor here. He was to change my working life dramatically. For the next 40 years, home or away, in Britain or abroad, I hardly missed an Albion game.

Chapter Seven

On My Travels – And Howe!

Ifelt I had a head start with Don Howe. I had known him as a player at the club and, in my youth, I probably idolised him. He had after all given me his shirt once after he played for the Football League against the Irish League. History may not be that kind to him as a manager, showing as it does that he took Albion from the lower reaches of the First Division to a place among the also-rans of the Second Division, without any of the cup success we had grown used to under Jimmy Hagan and Alan Ashman. But there was still plenty to admire about his work. He was ahead of his time with some of the advance planning that is taken for granted now. His former club Arsenal were the yardstick for everybody, still are in a lot of ways, and he brought a lot of the good habits that had helped make them double winners in the year he joined us.

At his side were two other members of Bertie Mee's backroom team at Highbury. George Wright came with the title 'assistant manager,' although he was more physio than no 2. He was a very good physio but wanted a job description that was wider reaching. Brian Whitehouse, one of Don's Hawthorns team-mates from more than a decade earlier, was a West Bromwich boy and was installed as our new coach. The differences in working practices soon became obvious. George was very particular, wanted things done right and insisted everywhere was clean and spotless. He taught me a lot because I was getting more involved with the first team. Standards were high and I'm grateful to him. His attitude rubbed off on me.

The change of management wasn't such good news for Tom Jones, the white-haired physio who had arrived from Birmingham City during Alan Ashman's time. Tom lived in Park Lane or Camp Lane, not far from the ground, and wasn't the sort to run on the pitch treating players. That role would have been left to Stuart Williams under Alan. Tom wore a white coat, as Fred Pedley had before him, and was more one for working behind the scenes. He fretted about his job when Don came and became more involved with the reserves than the first team. I'm convinced the worry over his position brought on his cancer. I felt for him with George coming in but Don wanted a second Arsenal, with the reserves and youths having a separate coach and physio. George brought a trainee physio to look after our youths. Tom was with the second team and, when he passed away, the trainee Richard Roberts became George's assistant – and later went to QPR as first-team physio. This was the Arsenal way, with each team in the club having their own staff, as the academies do now. But very few were doing it then.

My role changed as well but for the better. Don wanted me travelling with the team, so I felt part and parcel of the squad, climbing aboard the coach to all the games, home and away, as well as abroad. He seemed to have been everywhere with Albion, Arsenal and England, and I was thrilled to be taking a few small steps in his tracks. When we were on the road, he and George didn't like me to go down to the ground early with the kit. Unlike the practice in recent years, they insisted we should all arrive together and I had help unloading the skips off the coach. The players mucked in and Don and George felt that took their minds off the game for a few minutes. It was just one of their principles. Another involved the laundry methods. Don didn't like the way the local Co-op washed the match shirts, so Carol and me, plus the groundsman Stan Darby and his wife, did them all. We'd wash them at night, take them to Spring Road next day and earn a little extra in the process.

As for other changes behind the scenes, George brought in a retired contact of his to be in charge of the x-ray department, so examinations were immediate. We had two club doctors – Roy Bottomley and Roger Rimmer. It was Roy who taught Carol to play croquet at a garden party at Bert Millichip's house when Bert was chairman in the 1970s. Roy's surgery was a bit further down towards Albion from the chemist's where she worked opposite the West Bromwich office of the Express & Star. We also had a club dentist, Doug Barker, who was always in attendance and whose practice I still use. Dave Cooper, one of his assistants, eventually took over. Dave, who is a relative of our neighbour Margaret, is a Wolves fan and in more recent times when we won promotion and they didn't, I went for my check-up and was able to joke with him about hoping he wouldn't take his frustration out on my gums.

I believe Don tried to create a second Arsenal. He adopted a lot of good things from the Highbury model but I don't think you should want to be second to anybody at doing something. It's better to be the first at something else. I think he should have done more on being innovative at West Brom. There were probably things you could do at Arsenal that you couldn't do at Albion, for whatever reason. As ever, results dictated the mood and he had a difficult time on the pitch. Jeff Astle was out long term with injuries and young players like Len Cantello and Asa Hartford had to gain experience in a side who were often struggling. I didn't think his tactics were the best, in as much as he moved Tony Brown up front. That wasn't Bomber's game and he didn't like playing there. It just didn't work. He preferred being in midfield and pouncing from deep because that's how he scored most of his goals. He was unsettled at one point under Don. Can you imagine if he had been sold in his prime? Thankfully, he stayed to score another 100 or so goals in Albion colours.

I think it was in Don's time that we had the weights room built at the back of the gym at Spring Road. Training was intense, with lots of weights, medicine balls and running. He was very big on the fitness side and some senior players found it extremely hard. The stop watch often seemed to be in his hand. I remember him taking the team to Oldbury – I think it was Newbury Lane Sports Centre – and it was run and run and run. The idea was to check the lads' recovery time. They were pushed so hard, they would literally be sick. George would be taking their pulse or whatever and checking how quickly the heart rate got back to normality. Another time, we went to Hadley Stadium for a superstars competition that Ray Wilson won quite easily. And I'm not saying that because he is Scottish and there was a cash prize on offer. In an effort to sharpen them up, the players were weighed every Monday morning and I've known Asa and Len put their fingers down their throat or take a laxative if they had had a particularly good weekend. Managers like players keeping the pounds off but that way is definitely not recommended.

Once I started travelling with the team, one of my jobs was planning for the return journey by going to the shop down Halfords Lane and collecting items like turkey legs, boiled bacon sandwiches, slices of onion, black pudding, tomato, fruit cake, cans of Albright ale, tea and coffee. Now, it's all pasta and ready-cooked meals for the microwave. So professional did we become that George and our commercial manager Les Thorley were sent to vet the hotels we would be staying at in the months ahead. They would check that the beds were big enough and the food was all right. They would give the kitchen staff menu guides and assess the distance from a hotel to the ground. It was all forward thinking and homework. A lot of the top-flight clubs do this now but took a long while to catch up. Pre-match, the players tended to have cornflakes with syrup and either tinned fruit or poached egg – a combination of sweet and light. That was a complete change. Boiled chicken or poached egg on toast had previously been the choice, with steak, possibly, a few years earlier. Willie Johnston liked his lamb chops when he first came down from Scotland but I'm guessing he fell into line pretty quickly. There was a mix-up on a trip to Hartlepool during our Third Division days much later and the hotel interpreted our request for a nice hot soup as meaning we wanted something spicy. None of the players could stomach it but kept straight faces when Norman Bodell turned up late, none the wiser, and took a big gulp. His face just went redder and redder. I remember Don Howe asking me once in the 1970s if I was okay with the food. Not having to be anything like as concerned as the lads with physical condition, I could have indulged a little more but I said: "If it's good enough for the players, it's good enough for me." "Right answer," he said. "Well done!" He didn't want anyone rocking the boat.

I'm sure we were welcome back at hotels. We always tipped the waitresses, waiters, coach driver; everybody who played a part in the operation. It's a bit different to recent years, I'm afraid. There were fun times as well. On a Friday night away, we would often all go to the cinema and 'Last Tango In Paris' before one game at Orient in the Second Division springs to mind. I can remember going to one venue which was like a two-screen picture house and George approached the window to book the tickets for everybody. The woman said: "I'm sorry but it's the next window down," so George moved along a few feet thinking he would be seeing someone else, only to encounter the same woman. We all thought it was hilarious.

I found my new hands-on role a challenge but an exciting one. I have a photo taken of Don, George, myself and our substitute Roger Minton in the dug-out at West Ham on the opening day of the 1971-72 season – our first game under new management. It was also my first League match on the road as part of the official entourage and I'm struck now by how close the spectators were to us; also by my decision to wear a collar and tie. We won with a Tony Brown goal – some things weren't changing – and we emerged unscathed, so the locals must have been good-natured with us. I always sat on the bench and had a bag containing spare studs of different lengths, pliers, pinchers; everything for an emergency because often the dressing room would be locked for security – or that's what the home club would tell us.

The actual schedule was an eye-opener, especially if we had two away games in the space of a few days. We went to Newcastle and Stoke with only 48 hours in between at the end of Don's first season and Leeds and Newcastle ring a bell as another back-to-back assignment, possibly from the following season. If it was, say, a Wednesday-Saturday double-header, we would generally leave The Hawthorns on match-day morning. The players would have lunch, go to bed in the afternoon, play the match, then return to the hotel to stay the night. Don and George thought that gave us the best chance of a quick recovery. When Arsenal won the double, they apparently rested and slept as much as they trained, so recuperation was a big thing. Next day, we would travel back to West Bromwich after breakfast for a light training session. If we had a substantial journey again for the Saturday, it would mean a very quick turn-around for me and another night away, this time on the Friday. Obviously it would be a lot easier if we, say, played in blue and white stripes in one game and our change kit in the other. But the packing certainly had to be done in a hurry. It was all go, go, go but it was enjoyable because my job was a lot more interesting. Would I have wanted to stay for 50 years had I not been more involved and going to away games? I'm not sure.

Don was very good with his staff. I can't speak too highly of him from that point of view. When he was appointed, we were saving up to get married and he always wanted to reward staff for the hours they put in. I remember Tuesday and Thursday night training for schoolboys at Spring Road and he wanted me there to make sure the balls were blown up and to look after the parents by making a pot of tea and seeing to anything else they required. I was basically on call to ensure everything ran smoothly. Ken Hodgkisson would sometimes be there until 11pm and then take mums and dads home, no matter where they lived. Parents used to say they didn't get that sort of treatment at other clubs. Don was very professional on that side of things. And, of course, having asked us to put in the extra hours, he encouraged us to claim for working unsociable hours and made sure we got more in our pay packets. That helped, with the big day approaching for Carol and me. We had been going out for three and a bit years and become engaged one Christmas time. I would like to say the proposal was made with me on one knee, amid a really romantic flourish. I suspect the reality was different but I did my best and had a diamond platinum solitaire ring made in the Jewellery Quarter in Birmingham by a friend or neighbour of John Talbut's. On the day we confirmed our long-term commitment, I appeared with the ring, a bunch of flowers and a bottle of champagne at a time when Carol had been ill with flu. I may have needed to remind her that Big T had played at centre-half at Wembley on the day of our first date. She was after all the daughter of an RAF flight sergeant, who had taken her on only occasional trips to The Hawthorns.

The house hunting followed and we had a lucky break when Carol talked me into a change of routine one Saturday lunchtime, when I was keeping an eye on the watch because of that day's home reserve match. She persuaded me to pop into Birmingham with her and, when she went into Marks & Spencer, I waited outside, bought a mid-day Evening Mail and noticed a house for sale in the small ads. We went to look at it that night. Actually, we had my dad to thank because I was all for having tea first and then popping over but he insisted we should go straightaway. It's a good job we did. He had been over in the afternoon for a look and told us when we saw him after the game that it might be just what we were looking for. It was as well we followed his advice and treated it as a matter of urgency. Surprisingly, there was no 'for sale' board up and we learned from the owners that the advert hadn't been due to go in the paper until the following week. As we were looking round, another couple appeared and said in no time that they were prepared to commit themselves there and then by writing a cheque. We quickly showed how serious we were as well and fortunately the owners insisted we had first refusal as we had turned up first – as long as we were also prepared to leave a deposit. We hastily handed over either £20 or £50 to secure the purchase. It was fate really. If I hadn't taken the unusual step of going into Birmingham on a match-day morning, or if I hadn't bought a paper or if I'd followed my instincts and put my stomach before our future by having tea at the normal time, we would have missed out. With Halesowen as our chosen place of residence, we moved on to the next item on our 'to do' list. By another happy turn of events, one of the directors had a printing firm in Spon Lane, West Bromwich, so we had all our wedding invitations done there. If I remember right, he wrote off the bill as a present to us.

Don gave me permission to miss an early-season game at Huddersfield in 1971-72 to get married. The service was held at St Peter's on Bloxwich Road in Walsall – the same church where Carol's mum and dad had married. My elder brother Frank (my only sibling) was best man and the reception was on the other side of town at the Three Crowns on the Sutton Road. From Albion, Alan Ashman's secretary Margaret Limbrick and her former colleague Janet Willetts (later Janet Thompson) were present. There would have been various matches in the club in those days on any Saturday, so the turn-out was smaller than it would have been in the close season. Perhaps we planned it as we did to keep the costs down. Or were there some tax benefits? The big day was September 11, 1971. It was 9/11 long before that date became fixed in our memories. The sickening terror attacks on New York and other parts of America were to come on our 30th anniversary but there were no thoughts of us taking to the skies to celebrate our marriage. We didn't have a honeymoon. We had received the keys to our semi the day before the wedding and had so much to do. It's the only property we've ever owned and cost £4,950. I can remember applying for the mortgage at the West Bromwich Building Society, where one of Albion's directors happened to be on the board. Although nobody ever said anything, I felt deep down that we got a mortgage thanks to him. Our wages weren't the greatest and I remain very grateful for being given a hand with this first – and only – step on the housing ladder.

We wouldn't buy anything until we had saved for it and could afford it. We didn't believe in borrowing, other than the mortgage. I was old-fashioned in other ways as well. Many years later, I was the last person at the club to be paid in cash. I had a bank account but dug my heels in and didn't let on I had. In my eyes, I was working for the bank if my money went in there. I insisted it was my right to be paid the old way and they used to come back from the bank with a bag of petty cash and my wages. Albion sent me an official letter eventually, offering to loan me money if I was short. Pressure on me to move with the times had come when a load of money disappeared from a car used to fetch the wages from the bank. The employee driving it had been buying cigarettes from The Hawthorns pub. Finally, I had to fall in line but I held out as long as I could. I was a stubborn so and so and felt justified when I got a parking ticket while queuing in the West Bromwich Building Society to make a deposit. It felt as though being paid by cheque was costing me money. The irony is that Carol wished long ago she could have been paid by direct transfer. She's the enlightened one of us. She sorts out all the bills and it's only in the last year or two that I've asked what we have to pay and when – in case I ever have to take charge. I've also recently got a credit card for the first time. I always used hers.

Chapter Eight

A Changing Of The Guard

My horizons altered in different ways after Albion finished comfortably out of trouble in Don Howe's first season. Carol had been to Italy once before with her family and knew Scotland because her dad was from up there. But I was breaking all kind of new ground in the summer of 1972 when the two of us went touring north of the border. We headed up the west coast and I loved it so much I found myself stopping the car every five minutes to take photos. Later that summer, I went on a plane for the first time when we went back up to Scotland for a friendly against Hibernian but my first foreign holiday wasn't until well after the girls arrived. That was to the south of France in about 1986 – the first of two or three trips we had there. I count myself lucky I've travelled to many parts of the world since, largely through football but also on holiday. I've always regarded travelling as a treat because finance and convenience made us favour places like Swanage and Exmouth for holidays when our family first started to expand.

Things were difficult on the pitch after the decision to do away with our change strip of plain yellow shirts and dark blue shorts. In their place, we adopted yellow shirts, with a green trim, and pale blue shorts. But we certainly weren't playing like Brazil and were in big trouble at the mid-way stage of 1971-72 before recovering very well. It was a period of transition. Someone was eventually going to end some great Albion careers and the task came on Don's watch. He waved off Bobby Hope and John Kaye, and John Osborne and Tony Brown stopped enjoying their football. One of the biggest stories of that season was the transfer that wasn't involving Asa Hartford. It was only when he went to Leeds to sign for them that it was discovered in a medical that he had hole in the heart. The deal was called off and a distraught Asa came back to The Hawthorns. The reporters and cameramen were outside hoping for a glimpse of him and I had to smuggle him out in a small van that used to be parked inside the ground. Don said: "Take him up the road to the hotel and make sure he's not seen." So Asa got in and lay flat on the floor. I opened the roller-shutters and drove him away. Everyone feared his career was over in his early 20s and Don did ever so well for him. The newspapers were queuing up for the story and he got the best deal he could for him. Whether the paper asked for its money back, I don't know, but Asa was playing for us again in no time and went on to play hundreds of more games at other clubs. Thank goodness he was able to carry on.

Lyndon Hughes was another to suffer an unusual condition. He had to have a kidney removed and everyone was worried about his career. But it didn't hinder him and he had a decent run with Don, as did Alan Merrick, who mastered the art of tackling not only with all his body weight but also with his shoulder. More than once, opponents had their nose displaced and referees were left wondering how it had happened. There weren't so many cameras around then. Under Don's management, there was a definite changing of the old guard and even the relatively young Alistair Robertson had his nose pushed out of joint for a while in the mid-1970s as Dave Rushbury emerged with considerable promise. Dave was quick enough to correct any mistakes but fell by the wayside after one good run in the side and went on much later to become a physio. I met him again when we played a pre-season friendly at Chesterfield. Keeper Bob Ward followed a similar course and has been at Chelsea and Middlesbrough, the latter during the reign of Bryan Robson, who was one of his contemporaries when he played a few games in our goal.

Full-back Trevor Thompson was the smallest apprentice I've ever seen but filled out and had a career at Lincoln after a few games with us. I believe he was once taken to a London bone specialist to see how much he was likely to grow. Joe Mayo, who Don had back for hours in the afternoon to make him a better-than-average sort of centre-forward, was given his debut in our stay in the Second Division. He did okay and became a regular either side of us winning promotion and went to play in Hong Kong for a spell later on after being moved on to Leyton Orient. I met up with him when Albion went out to the Far East under Johnny Giles in the 1980s. Big Joe is still a regular at the player reunions, where his jovial nature always makes him a welcome guest.

Graham Smith was one of Don's signings who didn't come off. He arrived from Colchester and was a bit on the short side for a keeper. One of his later jobs was with Adidas and he set out to make sure the players all wore their brand of boots. I had a nice little earner through painting the stripes brighter before every game so they would show up on TV and in newspaper photos. Some of the lads complained they weren't being paid, so they blacked them out again. I would use the word 'average' to describe some of the players Don backed with runs in the side. But he probably didn't have a lot of money to spend and just got the best he could. He certainly had successes as well. Bobby Gould's goals helped keep us up in his first season and we all know what a good player Alistair Brown became here, even if he flourished mainly under subsequent managers. Then there was Willie Johnston. He was Don's best signing by far and was a reward for the club's patience in the transfer market. It took a club record fee to prise him out of Rangers and first the deal was on, then it was off and finally on again. Thank goodness we didn't give up on him. He moved into the house in Sutton Coldfield that became available when Gouldy joined Bristol City and what a winger he was! Things didn't happen for him straightaway and the most surprising thing considering he had underlined his star status at Rangers by scoring twice in a European Cup Winners' Cup final, was the fact we had to wait ages for a goal from him.

Once Willie got into his stride, though, he was just wonderful to watch; genuine box office. In the late 1970s, he trapped the ball with his backside against Nottingham Forest when a long pass was played to him. Brian Clough had every respect for Ron Atkinson and the flair he cultivated here but he leapt from his seat to complain, saying it was disrespectful. "If anyone in my side tries to do that, they will be off quicker than they can imagine," he yelled. I had no part to play when Willie ran out for the kick-in wearing an extra bit of 'kit' on what was Bryan Robson's home debut in 1975. It was an end-of-season game against Cardiff with nothing much at stake and the fact that Don had just been sacked probably contributed to the more relaxed atmosphere. But Willie produced a clown's mask from up his shirt while he was trotting down the tunnel and was pictured by the newspapers in it as the lads warmed up immediately before kick-off. Several of the defenders speak of Don having improved their game but the wonderful legacy that was Willie Johnston was certainly the most redeeming feature of the Howe years.

Relegation was difficult to take, especially as we finished bottom, one place beneath Crystal Palace, and the atmosphere was very subdued for a while. More youngsters were seen at first-team level in the Second Division. Barry Donaghy was given a brief chance, a debut was handed to John Trewick and we saw a bit of Ian Edwards, who scored the strangest goal I've ever seen. Playing in the reserves at home to Manchester United, he headed in an opponents' goal-kick from inside the centre circle before the keeper could recover his ground. Brian Clarke, a young centre-back, was one some people had very high hopes of. I used to organise competitions for the young lads, like running, keepy-uppy, finding who had the longest throw and who could score from a corner. The prize was a week off jobs. Brian kept the ball up nearly 1,000 times once but still didn't win the competition. And obviously something was lacking in his general game because he didn't come through.

Don was sacked after we failed to win promotion in two attempts despite challenging each time. Gates had dropped dramatically and goals were in scarce supply, although Bomber hit seven in one week in January, 1974. Three came against Notts County in the FA Cup and four at Forest in the League the following Saturday. There was a story around that the Sherriff of Nottingham banned him by making it clear he wasn't welcome back in the city! Despite those high spots, it was inevitable Don would leave. I think he deserved more for the effort he put in. He did loads to overhaul the dressing room area at the ground and must have learned much from being with the great players who had won the FA Cup in 1954 and through playing with Bobby Robson. Don was a very good coach but I'm not so sure about him as a manager. There are some who are very good at someone's side but not so clever when given full control. Maybe he was in that category.

To fill the vacuum caused by Don's sacking near the end of 1974-75, our reserve manager Brian Whitehouse stepped up as caretaker manager and a young star came to the fore. Albert McPherson had probably done as much as anyone to oversee Bryan Robson's development and could always spot a player, which is why he has worked well into his 80s as a scout – for Middlesbrough among others. Brian would have seen all that potential as well and he named him for his debut in a win at York. A week later, Bryan scored on his home debut against Cardiff, then netted another at Nottingham Forest in the last game. Two goals in three matches....he was on his way. He may have missed out on playing for Don at first-team level but their paths were to overlap. In the 1980s, he worked closely with him when he was captain of England under Bobby Robson and Don was no 2. Margaret Limbrick, the secretary to four managers at Albion from soon after I started, would have been delighted with Bryan's progress. One of her duties was ordering a proper cooked meal for him in the Throstle Club after training to help build him up when he was just a boy. Brian Whitehouse's good work didn't go unnoticed either. He was still with us into the next decade and made such a good impression at The Hawthorns on Ron Atkinson that he was taken by him to Manchester United, who also eventually paid us a British record transfer fee for Bryan.

My elder brother Frank and I in our formative years. He shared our dad's love of mechanics rather than my passion for football. Sadly, he passed away at the age of 51 - the same age that my wife Carol lost her only sibling, Keith. Below: A place at Smethwick Hall Boys School was my 'reward' for failing my 11 Plus. At least I made it into their school team as the first step towards what I once hoped would be an Albion playing career. That's me to the left of the goalkeeper.

At our house with my dad Frank and mom Mary and probably quite proud of that hanging basket. Below: Two heroes from my early Hawthorns career, Derek 'The Tank' Kevan (left) and John 'Yorky' Kaye.

Above: The happiest of Albion days. Tony Brown and Bobby Hope, two of the Baggies heroes I can genuinely call good friends, hold aloft the FA Cup after one of the best finals of all time. Okay, I'm told it was quite a poor spectacle for the neutral but a wondrous strike from the left foot of Jeff Astle (below left) saw us home. Also seen above are (from left) Graham Lovett, sub Dennis Clarke and Doug Fraser. It was the second of our three Wembley outings in four seasons in a period we had kicked off by winning the last of the League Cup's two-leg finals. Wembley '68 was also my first date with Carol, so I was a happy chap doing my duties at The Hawthorns.

Those bostin' red socks again, this time on display in a 1969 League win away to a West Ham side containing Geoff Hurst, Martin Peters and all. But don't ask why we wore them at Wembley! Below: My own big match - marrying Carol in Walsall early in the Don Howe era in 1971.

Happy on our travels.....ready for take-off on one of our 1978-79 UEFA Cup trips. The two men to my right are Tom Silk, who was later killed in an air crash, and Alan Everiss - a man who knows a thing or two about long service himself. Below: A time for big hair and big collars obviously as I join Ron Atkinson and Colin Addison to see Bomber Brown receive yet another award.

Time for a nice cuppa! The tension of a tight cup-tie is eased by a brew-up for our clearly exhausted players. Preston were on the way to relegation to the third tier when they gave us a surprisingly tough time in a 1980-81 fourth-round League Cup tie that went to three games. I was on teapot duty before we finally edged through in extra-time. Below, one of my less pleasant tasks sees me accompanying the injured Romeo Zondervan back to the changing room.

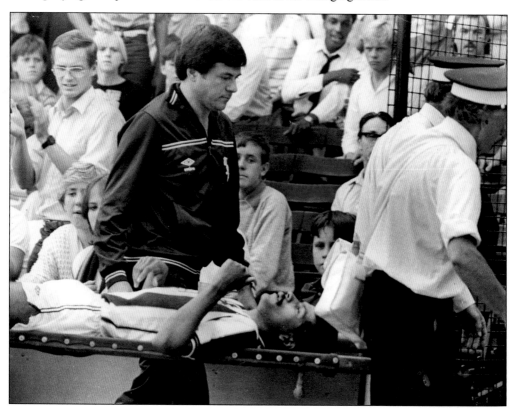

Above: Away with my 'home team'. All smiles on our first foreign family holiday, to the South of France in the mid-1980s. Below: Travelling further afield with manager Brian Talbot, scout Norman Bodell and physio John McGowan when we went to California in the spring of 1990.

A glimpse into my lesser-known part in Ron Atkinson's life. Left: Clare joins us as I prepare for chauffeur duties. Below: A spot of lawn mowing at Big Ron's place and, bottom, a reflection early in 2013 on how this souvenir from our travels had played a humorous part in dressing-room life.

Chapter Nine

The Style Of Giles

I didn't think I was going to be able to hack it with Johnny Giles. A few weeks into his reign as Albion's first player-manager, I was unhappy in my work, finding it difficult coming to terms with some of his methods and considering my future. I even went for a job at a sports shop in Dudley. I don't know if I really wanted it but I had an interview. When Bob Ward went to try to get the reserves' win bonus increased, he was told it was only the first team that mattered and that didn't go down well with me either. I had seen Johnny organising all these five-a-side games in training and it didn't seem right to me. It was different because, after all the running the players did with Don Howe, it was as if they weren't doing what they should be doing. The Albion supporter in me was flustered.

Training was more relaxed and more fun. It was all geared to their touch, control and movement. Johnny and his midfield partner Billy Bremner had caused us some pain over the years, especially at Elland Road, and he was still a brilliant player; good enough to be at the hub of everything in practice at Spring Road and on match days. He still demanded hard work and would stop a five-a-side game if the lads became sloppy or weren't vigorous enough in closing down an opponent. He would threaten to revert to hard labour if they didn't put the effort in and say something like: "Look, it's up to you. Do you want to do endless laps of the pitch instead?" He would tell them once, twice maybe, and that was all. There was a limit to his patience. Before his team talk at half-time in one game, he turned to a player – I have it in mind it was Ally Brown – to ask if he was all right. Did he have a knock? Was he feeling under the weather? When the answer to both questions was 'no, boss', Johnny said: "Get in the bath then if you think that's good enough." It was a warning to the whole squad about his high standards. The message got home and everyone knew what he wanted.

We had a very slow start in 1975-76 and couldn't win a game. In fact, we could hardly score. In three of the first four matches, we failed to come up with a goal and we had only one victory to show from our first 12 fixtures, including a League Cup defeat by Fulham at the first hurdle. Just as Giles was patient in possession on the pitch, though, he was prepared to bide his time with results and chip away to try to turn things round. He knew what he was seeking, even if it took a while. Gordon Nisbet tells how the gaffer looked daggers at him in a defeat at Sunderland when he hit a head-high pass to him. Gordon didn't play again. Alan Merrick didn't get further than appearing at Southampton in the first League match and experience was the order of the day, as it had been in the daunting Don Revie side that Johnny did so much in to make things tick at Elland Road.

England World Cup hero Geoff Hurst came down from Stoke and we would pick him up just off the M6 when we travelled north to places like Carlisle and Blackburn. I used to take him to the dogs at Monmore or Perry Barr but his impact on the pitch was minimal; a dozen or so games, a couple of goals and he was gone. I had already been present when Johnny leaned on his contacts in the Republic of Ireland by taking the lads there for two pre-season games and he delved into his past again to recruit two of his old international pals from there a few weeks into the season. Many people, me included, thought Paddy Mulligan was over the hill but what an acquisition he turned out to be. He hardly ever gave the ball away because he was an excellent passer and, although he was lacking in pace, he never seemed to get caught out. In front of him, Mick Martin had played for Manchester United and was the perfect player to be at Johnny's side. With a solid defence already in place, we had the basis of a good team.

The players responded superbly to Johnny's ways. They loved him. Everyone had been interested to see how it would work with a gaffer pulling the strings from the centre circle rather than the dug-out and it was quite a change. It was a totally new outlook and there were lots of fresh ideas. Gradually, I came round to his thinking and found myself agreeing with his philosophy. Before long, any thoughts I had of selling rugby shirts and cricket pads from a town centre sports shop were scrapped. I realised I had probably been naïve in doubting him and he's in my top three Albion managers, if not top. I've even recommended to various subsequent managers, including Alan Buckley when we were having a bad run, and suggested they should have him in for a month as help. They never did. I suppose it would have shown a big weakness. I know where I could have gone for someone to second my proposal, though. Bomber Brown loved Johnny's philosophy.

I suppose the Giles reign will be synonymous with the change strip we wore at Oldham on the day we won promotion – the yellow and green stripes, with light blue shorts. That change strip came in during the second half of Don Howe's time and lasted a few years, although we switched to green shorts when we were back in the First Division. The Brazil design had been ditched after we played at Preston one night and it became hard to distinguish our yellow and pale blue from their all white under the floodlights. One more subtle alteration of Johnny's that impacted on me was to have the shorts extended by two or three inches to give the players more freedom and movement. And, if I remember right, there was more tampering with the boots. The lads should have worn Gola but often preferred to wear Adidas ones, with the markings doctored as necessary

So what was the Giles way? He never talked about the opposition and believed in keeping it simple. "If we have the ball, they can't score" was one of his sayings. He was also happy to see the ball played across the back four as many times as was necessary before an opening for a forward pass was spotted. We would frustrate teams. He used to say that the side who made mistakes would lose. In terms of percentages, possession was 100-0 in our favour when John Osborne had the ball, so why make it 50-50 or 40-60 by having him kick it long? Johnny would receive a pass from the centre-backs and, if he couldn't turn, he'd give it back and they would become more confident on the ball. In many away games, the home fans would boo us for what they thought was our negativity but he wouldn't budge. Not even if we were two down. We won quite a few games late when opponents lost their discipline.

Giles and George Wright got on well together and it was a happy ship. The club weren't going to renew George's contract after Don Howe left but he stayed and was with us until the mid-1980s. Despite the Arsenal connection, George probably had a bigger influence on Giles than he had done with Don, so much so that he also went to work for him at Vancouver Whitecaps between Johnny's two Albion stints. They placed high demands on everyone to be prepared to put their foot in and be happy receiving and playing the ball. Johnny set out to make everyone feel comfortable on the pitch because he was being paid to shoulder the responsibilities and the worries. He didn't do the job because he had to. He didn't need the money. I think the fact he was always on the level – and never too high or too low – contributed in a big way to us turning the season round. From winning only one of our first 12 matches, we went 11 games without defeat, the win at Bristol City in late October being seen as the catalyst for our climb up the table. We didn't score that many but didn't need to with our miserly goals-against record and we did come up with one of the TV companies' Goal of the Season from Willie Johnston – a brilliant long-range shot on the run that won two points late on for us at Blackpool.

It wasn't all one way. At Luton shortly before Christmas, Johnny apologised to the players after being sent off in a 2-1 defeat. But he let on that he had been waiting for years to get one of their players (Ron Futcher) back in a private grievance. There was a players' disciplinary committee in place at the time and he was fined £25 by the lads – the same amount as if any of them had been responsible. And he promised it wouldn't happen again. He would always talk briefly about the game to the team when they returned to the dressing room and the door would stay shut, with a hand on the handle from the inside, to ensure there were no interruptions. When we won at Oldham to clinch promotion, the job of bringing about a few moments of squad privacy was mine and I needed a bit of strength and concentration to keep control because all manner of people were trying to get in. But Johnny wanted to finish his speech and thank the players for all their efforts and congratulate them on getting their just rewards. Then he gave me the nod. I let the handle go and there was a flood …..the chairman, directors, press, well-wishers. I hadn't got a chance of picking up any kit.

The dressing room at Boundary Park was long and narrow and we had our fair share of laughter in there. On one visit, George Wright chucked some cold water over the top of the toilet cubicle, thinking one of our lads was in there but, instead, out came a strapping 6ft policeman, dripping wet. That was one item of paperwork he might not have got finished properly. George's face was a picture but no-one said a word until the officer had gone, then we went into hysterics. On the afternoon we pipped Bolton to the third promotion place in 1976, the players went out into the stand to acknowledge the fans who filled the pitch. The place was awash with Albion supporters and the journey home was unforgettable. We didn't want it to end. Virtually every vehicle seemed to have an Albion flag or scarf from it and the motorways were one long snake of yellow and green, blue and white. Normally, the fans have long gone when we leave a ground but the invasion meant they left much later that day. There was even an old double-decker bus with an open doorway and some of our fans were swinging off the pole. The champagne was flowing on our coach as well. Goodness knows how much I drank. There were some fans waiting to welcome us at The Hawthorns, then I drove to Halesowen to bring Carol back for another celebration.

We were all surprised when Johnny resigned a few days later, although he was subsequently persuaded to stay for another season – one we used to consolidate comfortably in the top half of the First Division. In fact, we were pushing for a place in Europe until falling away in the spring. And it was all done without loads of signings. Our only new face until we signed David Cross towards Christmas was Ray Treacy. He lifted spirits as well as our goal output for a while. We played the Irish national team at Bisham at least once and would go afterwards for a meal at their hotel, which was actually more of a good guest-house. It wouldn't hurt more footballers to occasionally stay at that type of place rather than have the five-star pampering. At the meal, all the Irish lads would sing a solo, no problems, and Paddy Treacy would do a guitar piece. But none of our lads were so eager to get on their feet.

We had won the FA Youth Cup in the same month as securing promotion. We beat Wolves home and away in the final and Derek Statham was blooded in the first team late in 1976 at the age of 17 a few months later in succession to Bryan Robson and John Trewick. On his debut at the Victoria Ground, Derek produced a brilliant run from left-back and shot past Peter Shilton to open the scoring. The TV cameras were there and 'Tucka' Trewick sealed the points to make it a great afternoon for our young stars. Those were the days when we could beat Stoke. Thrashing Manchester United 4-0 and coming back from two down to hit four against Tottenham underlined what a decent side we were but there were difficult times as well. We lost 7-0 at Ipswich and Johnny's reaction was interesting. You might have thought the coach journey home would be horrific but we stopped twice on the way back to stock up; with beers for the players, and brandy and gin for the directors. It was Giles's way of getting a bad day out of the system. He would say his piece, then unite the players to do better next time. And we did. I see we lost only one of our next eight matches. On the way back from Suffolk, the players were telling the coach driver to slow down in the end as we hadn't polished all the cans off. The story goes that Ossie's wife woke him up the next morning with the message: "John, it's eight. John, it's eight." To which he replied: "Oh, bloody hell, no! Have they scored again?"

Another low point was the night Willie Johnston kicked the ref, or at least gestured to. Cloughie was in the opposition dug-out again but this time it was at home to Brighton, then of the Third Division, in the League Cup. We were two down and on our way out when Willie set off on a mazy run that took him past several opponents and into the area before his progress was halted by the referee getting in his way. He pretended to kick the official up the backside – no-one will ever convince me he tried to make contact – and the crowd broke into a chant of: "Nice one, Willie, nice one son." That probably didn't help because the linesman was stood there with his flag up and the ref's attention was eventually drawn to the fact something had gone on behind his back. By no means for the first time in his career, nor the last, I had to go and run the bath water for him a little earlier than planned and he was banned for six weeks. He had a very short fuse but he also had a heart. I've seen Willie confronted by young full-backs and he would pass the ball rather than go past them. I swear he didn't want to be the one to wreck their confidence. But he would do his best to run senior internationals ragged and some of his antics were outrageous. He was a lovable rogue and his disciplinary record was terrible but it wasn't through fouling. He just had no idea of how to count to ten and walk away when he was provoked.

Laurie Cunningham fell foul of another set of disciplinary standards after Johnny had signed him from Orient for £100,000. We were playing at Villa on a Monday night in our last match of the season and Laurie, despite a goal on his home debut and quite a few more soon afterwards, was already in the gaffer's bad books for reporting late for training that day. He said he had things to do in readiness for an England under-21 trip to Scandinavia but pushed his luck again by being late for the coach to go to the game. John had held up departure to wait for him but said to him as he got on: "It's okay, you can go back home." He told Laurie to get off and then said: "Carry on, driver." He was making his point that players had to toe the line. He instilled good habits. And Johnny already knew, as we all did, that this was going to be his last game in charge.

Chapter Ten

The Two Ronnies

Alison was approaching three by the time Johnny Giles departed and she found herself with a little sister just before his successor Ronnie Allen took the squad off to Spain for a couple of friendlies in the build-up to 1977-78. It's strange that Clare's birthday is during pre-season and Alison's is at the end of a season, our eldest having arrived during our first year down in Division Two. I hated missing their birthdays when they were growing up, so we sometimes rearranged the parties for a Sunday because of games. I was away for one of Alison's birthdays when we went to Canada and America under Ron Atkinson in 1981 and was in California when she was doing her GCSEs in 1990. Games fell on Clare's birthday a couple of times in the 1980s but they were home ones and I was generally lucky. It wasn't unknown for me to work six or seven days a week and I would like to think I was too professional to cut any corners. As they grew older and came to understand that Albion sometimes had to come first, they jokingly called me 'Uncle' because they reckoned they saw me about as often as they met a more distant member of our extended family. Fortunately, Carol was always very good at coping with them on her own. She learned early on to be independent as she knew she had to write Saturdays off, as far as I was concerned, for ten months or so a year. It's only in relatively recent times that international weekends have come along and allowed a little time off during seasons.

It was not only home life that became more fun in the late 1970s. The Hawthorns was a happier place to be as well. Johnny Giles didn't just leave us with a top-seven First Division team. He had also signed Laurie Cunningham and then added Cyrille Regis for a pittance, although Ronnie Allen had done the scouting of big Cyrille and made the recommendations that we signed him.

He had a good contact in the south who had tipped him off that a star was in the making down there. Ronnie was an Albion legend and a popular choice when named as the new manager – even more so when we started the 1977-78 season well and realised we had a couple of real jewels on board. Cyrille and Laurie were a breath of fresh air at the club and just added the goal-scoring power we had lacked for much of Johnny's time. With Derek Statham now established and Brendon Batson shortly to arrive, we also had a formidable defence. The likes of Tony Brown, Len Cantello, Bryan Robson and Willie Johnston were in front of them and things were about to take off. Cyrille banged in goals from the word go, some of them quite stunning, and we looked well placed for a good League Cup run in addition to our exciting League form before losing at Bury of all places on a horrible foggy, icy night. Then Ronnie departed to Saudi Arabia almost as quickly as he arrived and the board looked to Cambridge United for his replacement. Considering Don Howe had come from Arsenal, Johnny Giles from Leeds and Ronnie included Wolves and Sporting Lisbon on his CV, this was a change of direction. But any thoughts of it being a small-minded appointment soon went out of the window.

Ron Atkinson was as good as Hagan, Allen or Giles when he pulled his tracksuit on and joined in training games; or at least he thought he was. He didn't lack confidence. His playing career may have been spent mainly with Oxford but he would re-enact big games at Spring Road and he would be Pele. When we played Valencia the following season, he would be Kempes or Bonhof and he would be talking out loud 'give it to Kempes'. It was the youngster in him having a lot of fun but I'm sure he'd like to think he was the bee's knees when he connected with a good volley. He was a huge personality. Before long, of course, as we scored goals by the net-full in blazing a trail towards Wembley in the FA Cup, he was given the Champagne Charlie image by the media. Was it justified? Yes and no. He would entertain the press over a drink or two at the Europa after a game. They loved him and the relationship was very good. They saw a lot going on around the place but could be trusted over what to write and what not to write. On our trips – and there were plenty of those – the champagne corks were often popping among the staff before the plane had even left the tarmac. But he loved his cup of tea really. He used the image thing to his advantage.

Behind the scenes, a lot of the habits from Ron's predecessors remained in place. A hot bath, for example, would be run at the ground before matches for those who wanted it, home or away. A few were keen to jump in because they felt it got their circulation up. If I remember right, it was a practice started in Johnny Giles' reign, at the suggestion of George Wright. A dressing-room ritual I observed for years at home games concerned skipper John Wile. My job was to throw three balls to him shortly before the players went out. The one that felt best on his head was the one we would hand to the referee for the match. Inevitably, as we found success, Ron found himself in opposition to the managerial big guns in vital games and had a go at Cloughie once because our dug-out at Nottingham Forest was situated so far from the half-way line. "You might as well stick us in a boat on the Trent" was the gist of his message. Ron took his revenge when they were at our place at a time when the main stand was being rebuilt. It was a temporary dug-out, so far from the half-way line that it seemed to be by the corner flag. All you could see when you peered down the line for Cloughie were JCBs and tractors. During our 2-1 win, Ron yelled: "It's fuckin' great down there, isn't it?" There is a sting in the tail, though. As Forest manager many years later, Big Ron got his dug-outs mixed up at his first home game, against Arsenal, and found himself sat down next to Patrick Vieira and Dennis Bergkamp before realising his mistake.

Ron's stylish touches as Albion manager didn't just concern foreign jaunts. For away League games, we used to arrive at a ground at 2pm, having sampled some fine dining en route. His pre-match choice for the whole squad was rump steak, egg and beans. He took off whatever shackles there were and some of the football was scintillating. The 3-2 win at home to Manchester United on a mudbath of a pitch at The Hawthorns was one of the epic nights of my half a century there and made us well fancied for the Cup. We won another thriller at Derby in the next round and then put out Forest, who were on their way to winning the title. But we unexpectedly lost in the semi-final to Ipswich on a depressing day when John Wile's shirt needed an extra wash after he famously spilled all that claret in the club's cause. As we did for the FA Cup final ten years earlier, we had special shirts made for Highbury – it's a pity John's showed as much red as yellow and green. Ron was bitterly disappointed and wasn't happy with the TV people who had him pictured with the Cup at Wembley beforehand. He reckoned he was stitched up and didn't think he would be doing anything his counterpart Bobby Robson wasn't asked to do.

He didn't show a bad temper very often......not unless someone trod on his bunion, that is. I've got a pair of his trainers or boots that show how his foot reshaped the mould. His mood was generally good because we won a lot more than we lost and he was just cut out for the European football we qualified for by finishing sixth in the League in his first part season. He much preferred playing games to training anyway, so the extra fixtures didn't worry him – something he proved by signing up to any number of friendlies at home and abroad.

I didn't go on that long trip to China and Hong Kong in his first summer. The visit was a diplomatic exercise in a lot of ways and George Wright had the kit-man duties added to his schedule. It might have been tongue in cheek but Ron had used our game at Wolves a few weeks earlier to ask if their manager Sammy Chung fancied going along with the party as an interpreter. During pre-season, we were heading out of England again, this time to the four-team Tennent-Caledonian Cup tournament hosted by Rangers at Ibrox. Even with those two games in Glasgow looming, we stopped off on the journey up there to play another one – a testimonial at Motherwell. Ron was happy to help out but wore a puzzled frown after the Motherwell manager Roger Hynd, once a hard-man centre-half with Birmingham, had put his side's 8-1 defeat against us partly down to the fact that his players were deflated after they had been destroyed by Willie, Laurie and Cyrille in a pre-match sprint competition. It was a strange comment. We had attacking threat all through the side and the two Browns accounted for at least half our goals that night.

In turning out up there for Joe Wark, we created a quiz question for Albion fans. Who was our keeper against Motherwell? Wrong, if you said Tony Godden or even his stand-by David Stewart, the Scot we had at around that time. It was Bruce Grobbelaar. He went on for the second half. It might look like we dropped a right clanger by not signing him but we had Tony and I know Ron didn't consider the Zimbabwean to be any better at the time than Mark Grew. Alan Everiss suspected we wouldn't have got a work permit for Bruce then anyway and it was only after he had been with Vancouver Whitecaps for a while that he emerged a year or two later as the keeper Liverpool wanted to sign. It was actually at our training ground that the Vancouver coach Tony Waiters looked at Bruce before signing him. There was obviously something there. We did have one glimpse of those legendary madcap ways before Bruce departed. He went out for a reserve game at Derby with a mask – something Mick Martin is also reported to have done in China – and pulled it from his belongings in the net during a lull in play. Derek Monaghan tells me the crowd started laughing and all the players looked round to see that a 'clown' had taken up residence between the posts.

I will deal shortly with our 1978-79 UEFA Cup run but that was the season when we felt anything was possible. I certainly did. I bet on us to win the treble and had a decent run for my money, although I ended up well out of pocket. You never felt we would lose. Confidence was so high. We expected to win, wherever we went. A good draw was often seen as a letdown. What a comparison with a few years later when we would turn up somewhere and almost wonder how many we could keep the score down to. Ron would accept being beaten by a better team but found it hard to take if we let our standards slip or if someone got away with something they didn't deserve against us. Then you'd realise he was disappointed. The defeat against Red Star in the UEFA Cup quarter-final springs to mind from that category. Although we had to rely on some magic from Laurie Cunningham to pull us through games when the fixtures piled up on bumpy pitches at the end of the season, 1978-79 was tremendous. We had been top of the table in January and looked genuine title challengers with Liverpool and Forest. It was the season of the 5-3 victory at Manchester United, of course, which came a few days after we won at Arsenal. As a fund-raiser for the Three Degrees statue to honour Cyrille, Laurie and Brendon Batson, there was a reunion at The Hawthorns a few months ago of some of the players on both sides from Old Trafford and loads has been written and said about what is one of the club's most famous wins. True to form, Ron was quoted as saying he wasn't sure the success over United was even our best performance that weekend. He believed we were even better in the win in the snow at home to Bristol City a couple of days later.

The sensational story behind that victory was our snow boots. Ron had been to the Adidas place in France some time before, when our former keeper Graham Smith worked for them. He came back with a pair of moulded, studded, dimpled boots and shouted 'Put these on, big man,' when he saw Cyrille sliding around in training one frosty morning. The difference was noticeable straightaway and the footwear was given much closer attention and put on one side for a snowy day. When The Hawthorns was covered by a white blanket on New Year's Day, the Bristol manager Alan Dicks and his assistant Tony Collins were on the pitch with the referee and it was obvious they didn't want the game on. Then, all of a sudden, Bomber went flying past the group as part of his warm-up and said: "Gaffer, we want this on." Those boots were working. Ron was brilliant. He said: "Ref, Tony Brown has played 700 games. If he says it's fit to play, it's fit to play." John Trewick wasn't due to figure that day and Ron threw him out of the dressing room for daring to suggest the match should be postponed. Joe Royle had scored a hat-trick for Bristol against Liverpool just before but it was obvious he didn't fancy it one bit either. Ron said: "Joe, if you don't want to get injured, stand still." Inevitably, we won and won well. It was a superb performance. The media made a big thing of the boots and Ron enjoyed telling the TV people some bull about winter tyres and special grip.

We had hit ten goals in less than a week, with seven different scorers, and taken maximum points. In our next home game, we thumped Coventry 4-0 in the FA Cup. They were happy days. Ironically, the wintry weather cost us that season. From January 13 to February 24, we played only one League game and we were rusty for that when losing by the odd goal away to Liverpool, who were our top-of-the-table rivals. It wasn't through lack of trying that we didn't have games. Ron was in his element trying to fix up friendlies during the long freeze and used the good contacts he had in Oxfordshire from his time playing down there to accept an invitation to play a testimonial against Witney – a place that seemed to be a few degrees warmer than most of the rest of the country. Then, out of the blue, one of the journalists who covered our games happened to say that Brian Clough was looking for a game for his players, so Ron rang the player, Trevor Stokes, and asked if he minded his big night being marked by a game between us and Nottingham Forest rather than us and Witney. As Forest were reigning League champions and we were having a good go at taking their crown off them, there weren't any complaints. There was a decent crowd and Ron reckoned it was the most competitive friendly he had ever seen, although it finished 0-0. We were all presented with a blanket – the town is famous for producing them – and the one I received was draped over our bed for years.

As pitches deteriorated all over the country and we faced a huge backlog of League and cup games – a schedule made even worse by the run to the

UEFA Cup quarter-final and the need for no fewer than three FA Cup replays – we could never quite regain our form. Liverpool pulled away, as they often did at that time, and it was a sickener when we lost at home to Forest in our last game of the season. That denied us even the consolation of runners-up spot. We'd also lost at Tottenham in our final away match and still finished with 59 points. That would have been enough for us to be crowned champions two years earlier. Even so, third place was our highest finish in the top flight since 1953-54, so it was a great season. It was just disappointing because we might well have won something.

There was one blot on Big Ron's first spell with us and that was David Mills. Word has it that we spent big on him because the club had some money that the taxman was going to get his hands on. We made what we thought was going to be a good addition but he never clicked as he had when he was a goal machine at Middlesbrough. He flopped really, especially as we had paid a British record fee to sign him in the middle of the title challenge in 1978-79. I should also say that David was the unluckiest player around. If anything was going to happen, it would happen to him. Even in a gentle end-of-season testimonial game for Garry Pendrey at St Andrew's, he snapped his Achilles tendon. In training in Gothenburg on a trip to Sweden in the early 1980s, he collided with Big Ron's boot during shooting practice and broke his nose. Another time, possibly in Cyprus, he fell awkwardly, broke his finger and had to go to the military hospital. He must have dreaded touring. Even in Bahrain, against a team Ron reckoned we could have beaten by naming half a dozen of the hotel waiters in our side, we were losing at half-time and Millsy was the one who really copped it from the gaffer. We won five in the end.

David's life had a desperately sad aspect to it well after he left us. He had a serious road accident in the Tyne Tunnel in which his father died. In Ron's second spell as manager here, we were playing a testimonial for David at Whitby on the Yorkshire coast – even then, the gaffer loved a match, no matter how far. We shouldn't have played because I've never seen rain like it and the pitch was ankle deep in water and mud. But we took a full team and did our best for him. Before the game, Colin Addison and Stuart Pearson, who went on as a substitute, were debating whether or not a character in the distance was our one-time £516,000 capture. Ron didn't miss his chance. "Just throw him this ball," he said. "If it goes under his foot, it's Millsy."

No sooner had we built a team capable of challenging for the big honours than we started losing key men. Len Cantello went off to Bolton after having a testimonial and, even more damagingly, Laurie Cunningham, who had played out of his skin when we drew in Valencia a few months earlier, got his big move to Spain when Real Madrid came in. How could he say no? We did what looked like some decent business in return by signing Peter Barnes and Gary Owen from Manchester City in the same summer but the follow-up was an anti-climax and we finished in mid-table as well as going out of Europe at the first hurdle. You could be forgiven for thinking Peter wasn't always with it. He got burned after ignoring advice and sun bathing on a trip to Kuwait and I'm told he had to withdraw from an England match once because he had absent-mindedly arranged his wedding for the day of an international. When we were down in Oxford on a special training trip, he indulged his passion for fishing by disappearing from the hotel with his rod and setting up on the bank. He startled the fisherman next to him by asking: "What canal's this, mate?" It was the River Thames. It was probably on that trip that Ron was having a drink in a bar and heard Peter and Gary Owen talking loudly outside. He sent a bottle of champagne out to them without specifying who it was from and said to us: "If they drink that, I'll run the bollocks off them in training tomorrow."

I remember Big Ron giving a long team talk at a hotel in London once about how Peter was going to be the key man in a game at Highbury. He made a strong point of how Barnesy was to use both our flanks to get at the Arsenal defence and not concern himself at all with defending, which no-one thought he could do anyway. The gaffer was in full flow – until he realised Barnesy wasn't with us. Our enigmatic winger hadn't realised the schedule had been changed and Ron had brought forward the time of our walk round the gardens, our lunch and our departure because he was worried about the traffic being heavy. Gary Owen piped up: "I don't know why you're worrying, boss......he never listens anyway." The point was proved that afternoon. Barnesy, watching Football Focus in blissful ignorance in his room while he should have been listening to his instructions, played well and scored in a 2-2 draw.

It was in 1979-80 that Bryan Robson made the step up to the full England team. Coincidentally, considering the legend he became at Manchester United, he made his debut on the 22nd anniversary of the Munich air crash. A picture in his autobiography shows him being challenged at Wembley by another midfielder who played at Albion, the Republic of Ireland's Tony Grealish. Laurie Cunningham also played in the game. It wasn't our only brush with the England team. We once had a training break at Bisham Abbey, which the international side often used as their headquarters before games, and Ron took a few of the players off to a show in Windsor at night and introduced himself, John Wile, Bomber and Gary Owen backstage to Little and Large. Big Ron gave us another great season in 1980-81 thanks to our fourth-place finish and had obviously made a big impression in his three and a half years. The big call came for him and, sadly, he wasn't around to lead us back into Europe the following autumn. Our travelling didn't stop, though. In fact it seemed fitting that we should be on the other side of the Atlantic when he was first tipped off that Manchester United wanted him.

Chapter Eleven

Lovin' It In Europe

You don't have to be abroad to gather some good tales for an autobiography. We had a trip to Bournemouth for a mid-season break once with John Osborne appointed as social secretary. We all went to a show featuring Lenny Henry, who mentioned on the mic that we were in the audience, and Ossie got us an invitation backstage. Needless to say, the lads seemed to be more interested in the chorus line of dancing girls than exactly which part of Dudley Lenny was from. Making some mischief was too much of a temptation for me. Spotting some almost empty champagne bottles, I saw to it that they were filled up with water, then sat back to watch the results. One or two of the lads showed themselves to be perfect gentlemen by pouring a drink for the ladies – and were rather startled when the contents were spat out. It obviously didn't taste anything like Moet. I've never seen so many try so hard for so long for so little. Sorry lads!

I said earlier how football had taken me to some parts of the world that I would probably never otherwise have seen – and I have Ron Atkinson to thank for that more than anyone. He loved a trip and always preferred playing a game to training. Fortunately, the players felt the same. As if we didn't do enough travelling in 1978-79 with the UEFA Cup run, we hopped on a plane with Birmingham's players in the February and beat the freeze by touching down in Guernsey to play a derby friendly with a difference. Ron had been there a couple of times with Cambridge but this was something else. All that separated the big crowd from the pitch was a piece of rope but Blues manager Jim Smith, who had visited our hotel the night before for a drink, had something else to remember the occasion by. He banged his head on the corrugated roof of his dug-out and declined the offer of a shoot-out between him and Ron to find a winner after our 1-1 draw. "I'm not fuckin' going out there!" he said in his expressive way.

The UEFA Cup campaign was one big adventure. For the opening game, against Galatasaray in Turkey, Sid Lucas was despatched to vet the hotels but we still had our problems on arrival. Someone said the mice and rats were scurrying round in overalls and two of the press guys complained they had a bat in their room. The accommodation was poor – possibly the reason we had our pre-match meal in a pavement café. Because of past crowd problems, the game was moved 300 miles from our opponents' stadium in Istanbul to the Aegean Sea port of Izmir, where we had our shoes polished by boys at the quay-side. It was very cheap generally and you could trade an Adidas t-shirt or an Albion pin badge and you had enough to get a round of beers in. We became snarled up in some bad traffic on the way to the ground and thought our campaign in the competition was going to start with a fine. At one point, we were going to bail out and walk but decided that wasn't a good idea if there were one or two hot-heads among the locals in a crowd of nearly 40,000. Any fears of punishment were allayed, though, when we discovered the referee was in the vehicle in front of our coach. He was late as well, so there were no penalties. It was a terrific performance to win 3-1 there all things considered. Although it was quite fashionable in Europe at that time to go into an away first leg with a lot of caution, it would have been a waste of our talents for us to set out in a defensive frame of mind. We just played our natural attacking game and beat them well. We celebrated by going for a good meal but George Wright wasn't happy for some reason. He missed the dinner and I had the gift that had been allocated to him. That probably made him a bit grumpier.

The lads had organised a swimming competition among themselves in the pool in Turkey but Dr Rimmer opted for the ocean when we arrived in Portugal in the next round. He stripped off and plunged into the high waves when we went for a stroll. It was so rough that there was no-one else on the beach. What's that saying about mad dogs and Englishmen? Hand in hand with our brilliant League form – we lost only twice before Christmas – we just kept defeating whoever was put in front of us in Europe. We beat Braga home and away without conceding a goal and the lads were licking their lips at the prospect of a meeting in the next round with Valencia, who had a couple of stars from the 1978 World Cup finals in Argentina's Mario Kempes and West

Germany's Rainer Bonhof. We stayed at the Monte Picayo Hotel in the orange groves – complete with its own bull-ring and several pools. My room had a huge four-poster bed, a phone in the bathroom and bowls of fruit. I'd never experienced anything like it. It was just typical Ron, pure class. Everyone had the feel-good factor. It was the night Laurie sold himself to Real with his fantastic contribution but the enjoyment stretched beyond our excellent performance in a 1-1 draw. We also went to the magnificent Lladro factory, where the senior members of staff were each given a present. I remember our director Johnny Gordon rushing down to the front when he thought Dr Rimmer was going to have his gift. There was a bit of embarrassment as our hosts scurried round looking for an extra piece. Anything for a freebie!

The trappings weren't quite as impressive when we went back to Spain for a pre-season tournament involving Sporting Gijon and Laurie's Real Madrid. We had a fairground next door, with the big wheel almost right up against my window. And it's fair to say we were not expecting great luxury when the UEFA Cup resumed after a four-month break in the March. Before we set off for the first leg of the quarter-final against Red Star Belgrade, I was sent to a butcher's wholesaler to get some meat to take with us. Obviously, there were worries about what we would be fed over there, although we all look relaxed enough in our club blazers and ties on the photo of us disembarking our Aer Lingus flight. The Yugoslav food turned out to be fine and I don't think we ate ours.

Where there was real cause for concern was on the way home from our tie against Carl Zeiss Jena the following season. As we prepared to leave East Germany, I had to earn my money in a way I was never in a rush to repeat. We were on the plane and just taxiing towards the runway when my name was called out over the Tannoy with the message that I should go to the front. I was used to going up to the cockpit because one of my jobs was to carry the giveaways, one of which – perhaps a pennant – would be hung up by the captain and his co-pilot. But it soon became clear this was no time for pleasantries. The military were around with their rifles and were keen to check what was in our skips. I was the one with the keys and had a bead or two of sweat on my brow when I was told to get off and show them the contents of our luggage. More than ever, I was hoping the lads had put nothing inappropriate in there. Or if they had, I prayed it would be in with the dirty kit because nobody in their right mind would want to be around that for long. Fortunately, the authorities were soon satisfied all was in order and we were on our way with at least one lasting memory from what was a drab, colourless place. Before the second leg, the teams were lined up ready to go down the tunnel when we realised there was a colour clash. Carl Zeiss were in yellow and we were in our yellow and green – the same as we had worn in the first leg. It was a bit of a rush getting the blue and white stripes out of the kit room in time for the lads to change into. Carl Zeiss didn't want to upset their sponsors by not playing in a kit provided by the camera company.

Going to Holland for a three-match tour in 1983, we were worried about whether we were going to make it over the North Sea. We were in a 40-seater Fokker with twin propellers and one decided to give up over Norfolk. I was sat by the window and watched it grind to a halt. The flight crew might have stopped short of actually saying it was engine trouble but a message over the Tannoy announced that we were going to have to divert to Heathrow because we had a problem. 'Too bloody right we have a problem,' I thought. I've never seen such a long queue for the toilet. As we landed, you could see the fire engines and ambulances at the side of the runway. You know that applause you sometimes get when a holiday flight lands? It would have been justified that day. There was a lot of relief. We took off safely soon afterwards on a different plane and decided not to tell anyone back home because we didn't want to worry our families. But Carol was coming home on the bus and saw the headline 'Albion in mid-air jet drama' in the paper. Someone had obviously broken ranks. Ron Wylie was in charge and was later quoted as saying he was terrified.

The trip had its light moments as well. We were playing cricket in the hotel car park and got so much into it that someone from the hotel management came out and asked us to stop because we were preventing the cars coming in. When the ball got whacked over the fence, Gary Robson, who scored in the first two games of the tour, was the only one brave enough to go and retrieve it from a field of curious and probably hungry ostriches. We were in our double Dutch phase and had Martin Jol and Romeo Zondervan in our squad. I got on well with both. Zondervan later took flying lessons (obviously the Fokker scare didn't put him off) and became an agent. I've seen him at the training ground in recent years trying to do a deal or two. When Martin came back as manager of Spurs, he asked if we had a room he could use for a minute or two – he wanted a cigarette. Ally Robertson was keen to see him as well. I had a photo of the reunion in the kit room. Martin told me he had given his kit-man at Spurs a grand for Christmas but I swear that's not the only reason I thought once or twice I wouldn't mind having him as a manager. I always hit it off with him.

I also went with Albion to Tunisia, where we were in a hotel opposite a zoo, and to Kuwait, where we stayed on a huge boat that doubled up as the Marriott Hotel. We also headed several times to America and Canada. But my furthest trip was probably to Hong Kong in Johnny Giles's second spell. We played Ipswich away on the Saturday and flew to the Far East on the Sunday. It was decided Carlton Palmer would travel if we had three or four injuries and we did. Boy, was he gullible! During the flight, I was pointing out a line of camels to him from 30,000ft and he was taking it all in. He was always chatting away, even bending the ear of Alan Everiss and giving him the benefit of his advice on various matters. I said: "Carlton, shut up. Alan has been all over the world with this club. Just listen to him occasionally instead." Irritating or not, though, you couldn't dislike him and he was such an enthusiastic tourist. I found him taking a photo of his bedroom door at the Excelsior Hotel in Hong Kong. Even I wouldn't bother with a picture like that and I take loads.

That trip for a one-off game was a big one for me. I was physio because George Wright had gone back to West Brom from Ipswich with the injured players and the dirty kit. It was quite an eye-opener and I had to think on my feet. Alan Everiss would do his own thing on trips and Gilesy would go to bed early, so I kept receiving phone calls about training. And Steve MacKenzie presented me with a problem I hadn't expected by asking for some sleeping tablets. I dug deep into the medical bag to sort him out and he made a point of finding me out at breakfast, when he was full of life, to thank me because he had slept brilliantly in the end. "Cheers, Dave. I really needed those Mogadon." It was at a reunion about 20 years later that I came clean and told him the truth; I hadn't a clue where we kept any sleeping tablets, so I just gave him two Aspirins.

I thought the lads would lead me a dance during the game by going down for no reason and demanding my attention. If they had been particularly mean, they could have organised it so one went down in one penalty area and another in the opposite one. I was dreading it. I've been physio on two trips – Hong

Kong and Scandinavia – when there were so many 'injuries' beforehand that George had to stay behind at the club to treat them. I feared the worst because I recalled him once racing on to the pitch to treat Willie Johnston, who was clutching his face and covered in 'claret'. But Willie had simply bitten into a blood capsule as one of his wind-ups. George was shouting "I can't find the cut, I can't find the cut" as he surveyed the mess. Another ploy favoured by mischievous players – if we were winning and the pressure was off, I hasten to add – was of lying motionless on the ground while the physio sprinted from one side of the pitch to the other. They would be taking a sly peek, though, so they could jump up right as rain just before he reached them. But I didn't have to go on the pitch once in Hong Kong or Scandinavia.

I'm convinced there's something in that. If there's not a fully trained physio there, players just get on with it. Liverpool didn't always have one – Sammy Lee used to run on as a sponge-man. When I stepped into the role, I had a white gown which I wore on non match days. My mom put an Albion crest on it. It was my work overall and one of the players thought it was a good idea when a new signing was made for me to pose as a barber. I had the scissors and comb in the top pocket and the pretence would only stop when the player was sat in the chair with the cover on. The Hong Kong trip left me with other memories, especially about the wealth gap. Those living in the junks were the have-nots but I noted they still had their Sky dishes. There were also a lot of Thalidomide victims and I bought a picture from a guy who had painted it with his feet.

During Johnny's second spell with us, there was a trip with a difference – a two-game end-of-season jaunt to Barbados for the Albion All Stars. I didn't go but was happy to help out their secretary Geoff Snape with the skip and two lots of kit for the likes of Ally Roberston, Martyn Bennett, Gary Owen, Ally Brown, Graham Lovett, John Osborne and Campbell Crawford. Derek Kevan was their manager. Geoff got on well with Gilesy and used to pop in for a cuppa with him – much to the annoyance of the chairman Sid Lucas. It was a charity trip, sponsored by an airline in the Caribbean, and Garry Sobers was the guest of honour, so the players had to be well turned out.

Unlike that distinguished line-up, Simon Miotto never played a first-team game for us but was worth being retained by Gary Megson just for his clown value. In Denmark, I remember him doing more than just lighten the mood with his antics. He had the lads in stitches. I always made an effort to be part of the group ethic on trips. I was lucky to always have an interest in where we were staying and travelling but I probably lagged behind most on the nights out. I'm not a big drinker. Richard Roberts had the float for the beers in Gothenburg and, as a group, we were outdrinking the locals. Richard became loud when he had a drink and was known to sometimes have a go at the directors. Big Ron used to say: "Just get him back to the hotel." Next morning, though, he would be as bright as a button and my eyes were like slits although I had been restrained by comparison.

I'd often not bother to watch pre-season games. I couldn't stand them. I would find any excuse to stay in the dressing room and tidy the skip. Abroad, where we didn't know the people well enough to trust them with an unlocked dressing room, I'd stay in anyway to watch over all our belongings and perhaps pop out for five minutes out of curiosity. Not that we necessarily had to be overseas to suffer losses. Someone once helped themselves to the TV, videos and music tapes off the coach at Everton while we were out of sight sorting the kit. We had stuff stolen off the bus at Chelsea as well after a game when the driver went into the ground to try to help out. The manager's briefcase was among the items taken. You can't always keep a proper watch. There are usually loads of people around a ground. I have to report that a player succumbed to temptation and showed his light-fingered side on one of the Anglo Italian Cup trips in the 1990s. I can't remember whether it was the one to Brescia, where we played on a white carpet and our players and fans had a snowball fight at the end, but the incident occurred on the outward flight. Malcolm Cinnamond, the Express & Star reporter, had left his passport sticking out of the back pocket of his jeans as he leaned forward to chat to Kevin Donovan. Bob Taylor, of all people, wasn't going to miss a chance like that. It was like an open goal to him. He carefully helped himself to it and kept it until well after its disappearance had become apparent and we had got off the plane. By then, Malcolm had confided his misfortune to our director Clive Stapelton and been told he would probably have to stay in Italy for a few days to get another one. Clive and the other lads were in on it and watched Bob place the lost item on the carousel and make sure it trundled along untouched until Malcolm spotted it and realised he had been 'had.' The players fell apart and Bob uttered the words: "Welcome to Albion."

Money was the hot topic of debate on another trip abroad when we refused to leave because the home club wouldn't pay us. I can't remember where it was but it might well have been when Sid Lucas was chairman. The concern arose because the crowd had been smaller than expected. Trouble of a different kind flared on Mike McGinnity's first trip as a director. Colin Addison was in charge because Ron Atkinson was busy elsewhere, and we were in Portugal, where Pat Jennings guested for us and Terry Neill was trying to sell Astroturf and seating for grounds. We played on clay. Something kicked off among our players and I thought: I don't want to know. I turned the TV up and had no intentions of opening my door. The squad were a feisty lot then with the likes of Robert Hopkins, Andy Gray, Tony Kelly and Carlton Palmer. The physio Graham Doig was caught on the hop when Addo asked who started it and he named some names. That was him finished with the players. We were asked to leave the hotel and had to go up to Lisbon for the rest of our stay. Mike McGinnity, who was good friends with Big Ron and later played a part in getting him to Coventry, was apparently heard to say: "Is every trip like this?"

The directors were generally well looked after and sometimes had presents off the airline. We mere mortals had to buy duty-frees if we wanted anything to take home as a gift. Simpler pleasures prevailed in the mid-1990s when Alan Buckley was manager. We sailed to the Isle of Man for a pre-season tournament and had a mini island tour because he'd heard the ice cream was to die for. We went round the TT circuit. Our own version of white-knuckle fun was a race on the go-carts. The physio Paul Mitchell went to book it and, while he was there, sussed out which was the quickest car. The lads found out he had got himself an advantage and threw him in the sea, followed by all his gear. I loved it over there. It was like going back in time. We saw the pictures of Douglas Beach when it was absolutely packed in previous decades. It had obviously felt like abroad in those days. It looked tired and run down when we were there. We won the tournament and that meant we could have the best hotel if we went back to defend our title the following year. But we said we'd only go if we could train at the main stadium and we were denied that privilege.

The Isle of Wight was once on the schedule as well and we should never have played. The ferries had stopped running because of the weather but we played in ankle-deep mud. As I say, Big Ron would rather have played a game anywhere than train. In Bryan Robson's time as manager, we were heading for sunnier climes and there was a delay at an airport, so our goalkeeper coach Joe

Corrigan was sprawled out fast asleep. Next to him, we planted a label that read: 'What a way to treat a legend.' We made sure we got the photos of it and they were certainly more palatable over Sunday breakfast than one for which I had some unknown suspects to thank. Did I imagine this or did the girl in Boots look a bit embarrassed as she reached over the counter to hand me the pictures I had taken on one trip. I got outside and found one of them showed a big bare backside. Someone had got hold of my camera for a few fateful seconds and engaged help in an 'exposure' of another kind. Thanks lads!

My biggest mistake when we went to California for four games at the end of 1989-90 was not taking my driving licence. As a punishment for being unable to take my turn at the wheel, I was ordered to stay awake on a long car drive from Los Angeles to Las Vegas – and back – in order to make sure the driver didn't drop off. And it was all in a day; hundreds of miles of desert, with no change in the scenery. Brian Talbot was in charge and the scout Norman Bodell and physio John McGowan were in the car as well. Sam Allardyce was also on the trip. We travelled for six hours each way but still had time for a look at the casinos, the big hotels and booked a show at night for which we got changed in the car park. Brian had got the trip sponsored, so it wasn't an official one and there were no directors. He was very generous about putting his hand in his own pocket as well. A young keeper called Mark Ashton had been released but had to be invited back and come on to the trip after Stuart Naylor did his cartilage in an end-of-season game. Mark couldn't believe it when his first game as a first-team player was against Real Madrid. I suppose it wasn't surprising we lost 6-1. Hugo Sanchez scored at least three and, when they fetched him off midway through the second half, the ground emptied. Clearly, the spectators weren't as turned on by watching Darren Bradley and Craig Shakespeare. Cans were being thrown on when Real had a couple of goals disallowed, although they were several clear by that stage. Vasco de Gama and Cologne were also there and we were the fodder to make sure Real got to the final. The trip wasn't confined just to this tournament. We also played a match in Arizona that was delayed because it was so hot. It may be commonplace now but it was one of the first times I remember seeing players coming off for drinks during the game.

I have had three trips to the States and should have had a fourth in 2011 but for my cancer diagnosis. The one with Ron Atkinson 30 years earlier had a spanner thrown in the works because there was snow around before our final League game at Leeds and concern arose over the fact the rearranged game was very close to when our flights had been booked for. But we made it and played matches in Portland, Vancouver and Edmonton, then had some leisure time in Florida on the way back. I remember Ron having a go on this automated bucking bronco in a bar in Fort Lauderdale. He lasted longer than some but not as long as he thought he would. It was during that stay he learned he was wanted by Manchester United. The tip-off came from Frank Worthington when they met at a function. Ron had a call on the same subject shortly afterwards from Joe Melling of the Daily Express – a familiar face on the Midlands beat – and the wheels were in motion. How could he say no to Old Trafford?

Chapter Twelve

Kit Fit For A King

My favourite Albion kit is the one we wore under Big Ron. Maybe it's because we had such a terrific team and the sight of them pulling it on holds happy memories. But the main kit didn't change greatly over my first 20 years at the club. The stripes became much broader in the Don Howe era – and stayed that way for a long while – and we dabbled with striped sleeves at times in the 1960s as well as having navy socks for a while much later. One surprise is that the throstle visible on our specially made shirts for the 1968 FA Cup final wasn't there before and wasn't to be seen for a long time afterwards either. Commercialism wasn't a big thing in my first two decades. But all of that changed in Ronnie Allen's second spell and our shirts were never the same again after the arrival of sponsors' names on the front for the first time. First we had BSR, then Swan through the connection with Jim Cadman (a family friend and the entrepreneur behind the Three Degrees Statue) and any number of others since. There were other cosmetic changes along the way. Numbers appeared on our shorts in 1969-70 and the throstle took up its perch on the left breast of the shirt the season after. As for our much-loved all white kit, that was replaced as a change strip by yellow shirts and blue shorts, although we were seen again in our Wembley garb, right down to those 'bostin' red socks, in one game at Chelsea. One other experiment was the use of navy shorts with our first-choice shirts. They became seen on occasions in away games if there was a partial colour clash but we enjoyed playing in them in our 1978-79 UEFA Cup run, so much so that we even favoured them in some home ties.

Ron Atkinson left us with another European campaign to look forward to when he departed and Ronnie Allen must have thought he had unfinished business here. But his first season back in charge was a strange one. He was very down after we went out of the UEFA Cup against Zurich Grasshoppers at the first hurdle. We missed so many chances over there that he was convinced we would turn it round at home. I remember him saying to someone: "We'll thrash you at our place." It was out of character for him to be so outspoken and he lived to regret it. We lost 3-1 at The Hawthorns to crash out 4-1 on aggregate. I'm glad I gave the cuckoo clocks a miss. It was a tie we wanted to forget as soon as possible. With Bryan Robson and Remi Moses following Big Ron to Manchester United around the same time, we nearly went down that season. And we remained a 'nearly' side in another way. In both the League Cup and FA Cup, we reached the semi-final but lost both.

There was an unusual occurrence at the Gay Meadow at the start of the League Cup run when both our blue and white stripes and the yellow and green alternative were adjudged by the referee to clash with Shrewsbury's amber and blue stripes. Fortunately, we were able to borrow their change strip of red shirts and white shorts in a throwback to what we had sometimes worn on our travels almost 20 years before. This 'loan' of kit wasn't a one-off. At Plymouth in the late 1980s or early 1990s, we had the bizarre experience of playing in QPR's red and black hooped change strip because both our strips would have clashed with Argyle's. The arrangement was facilitated by Scoreline, who supplied both us and Rangers with our kit. Under Don Howe, we had to wear Leeds' yellow and blue change strip at Elland Road at the start of one season – their initials are clearly on show in the photos. I can't clearly remember the sequence of events but maybe we had just taken our blue and white, assuming there would be no problem. Our own change at the time was a similar yellow and blue to Leeds'.

If I was a shade embarrassed at Elland Road, my mood was different in Ronnie's first summer back. I was miffed not to be taken along to Spain for a pre-season tournament and took out my frustrations in a constructive way. The old Halfords Lane Stand was being demolished to make way for a new one and I asked the chairman Sid Lucas what was going to happen to the lovely oak panelling in some of the guest rooms. I asked if I could have a few bits and pieces. He said it belonged to the demolition company, technically, but gave me the nod and I had all the panelling out of the boardroom and tearoom. It took us a few nights to do it but, with the help of my brother Frank and a low-loader, we got there. I asked around for someone to buy it and eventually it went to some heritage people in Cheltenham. Some of it was 17th century wood. We took at least eight solid oak doors and the oak handrails from the stairs leading to the directors' box. Apparently it had been destined for America. So not going to Spain did me a favour......I earned a handy few quid on the side.

It wasn't Del Boy skills I needed a few months later. It was the phone number of as good solicitor. I inadvertently contributed to one of our players being banged up in a cell before a huge cup-tie. Derek Monaghan was on the fringes of the side in the early 1980s and bought some tickets for his mates before we went to Tottenham for the second leg of the League Cup semi-final in 1981-82. But injury ruled him out and he travelled to the game instead with a friend of mine, Stuart, having bought the tickets for mates who decided in the end they wouldn't go if he wasn't playing. I passed them a couple of comps through the railings and they thought they would try to recoup some of their outlay by selling the leftovers. They were hardly trying to cash in – they were flogging £4 tickets for £2 a time – but it was because of their generosity and the crowd that quickly gathered round them that that police were tempted to move in. They were arrested, taken to the local station and kept in for a couple of hours, running back to the ground just in time to see Spurs score the only goal of the tie. The big irony was that Derek could have taken the tickets to one of the offices at White Hart Lane to get his money back, as Brendon Batson did. They were duly charged with obstruction and taken to court but won their case. The trouble was that they ran up legal costs of around £300 and their fine, if they had pleaded guilty, would probably have been about £20.

Another funny thing happened at Tottenham in that era. Derek Statham feigned an injury so he could race off to answer a call of nature. The crowd went mad because the ref even held the game up while the toilet door was bolted in the bowels, if I can put it that way, of the stand. Derek couldn't go as it happened but another player, a lad who never made it past the fringes of the side, had no such trouble in a reserve match. And he didn't even make it back to the dressing room in time. I'll spare his further embarrassment by withholding his name but, sufficient to say, his kit was never handed over to the laundry ladies. I had the unpleasant task of burning it. Losing the semi-final second leg at White Hart Lane wasn't our only big disappointment of 1981-82. We also lost by the only goal when the semi-final of the FA Cup took us to another part of London to face Terry Venables's Queens Park Rangers. Highbury held bad memories from 1978, when we didn't really turn up against Ipswich, but we hoped for better luck against Second Division opponents. We played in blue and white stripes this time and the lads looked really smart as they stepped into the sunshine in blue, white and red tracksuit tops for what was then a record 19th appearance in an FA Cup semi-final. We had more than 20,000 fans there, many of them at the Clock End rather than the North Bank we had been allocated four years earlier, but the outcome was depressingly similar. A clearance from Ally Robertson 20 minutes from the end cannoned past poor Mark Grew off Clive Allen and we were out again.

Ronnie Allen's last act was to keep us in the First Division at the expense of Leeds because we had hurtled down the table alarmingly while doing well in the cups. We were in big trouble until beating Leeds in our final home game and sending them down instead. Ronnie stepped aside again that summer but we had by no means seen the end of him. Into his later years, he used to come in to help out with the coaching, and impressed the lads with his shooting and penalty taking. He travelled to away games and even flew with us when we were playing in the Anglo Italian Cup. On a domestic trip, he once had the misfortune to be forgotten after travelling on the coach to Grimsby. The directors went by car and we thought there was an arrangement in place for him to go back with one of them. Half an hour into our journey, the phone went to tell us Ronnie was still at the ground and Grimsby's officials were getting ready to lock up. We had to turn the coach round and go and fetch him. The players were fuming.

We were entering a period of quicker turnover with our managers. The hot seat was becoming ever hotter. We had four managers in the 1960s, four in the 1970s and seven in the 1980s, including three spells by men who had been in the post before. The greater upheaval reflected the decline in our fortunes on the pitch. First, as we struggled to hang on to the coat tails of the leading clubs, Ronnie Allen and Ron Wylie lasted two and a half years between them, then, as we plummeted out of the First Division, Nobby Stiles (drafted in by his brother-in-law Johnny Giles) was in charge for no more than a few months before being succeeded by Ron Saunders. Not only did we drop back into the Second Division, we even worried about whether we were good enough to survive in it. As we started visiting some less familiar haunts, we went to

Millwall in the League Cup in Wylie's time and his coach Mike Kelly got stuck in at half-time to a young locally born defender called John Smith. True, we lost 3-0 (before winning the second leg 5-1) but Mike slaughtered him by saying he had no scars on his face and was a pretty boy. I felt sorry for him. Mike picked on him. It was John's only game in the first team. As for the Giles magic, some good players fell way short of expectations in his second spell. Imre Varadi, for example, couldn't handle the training under him because he was used to running and running and running with Howard Wilkinson at Sheffield Wednesday and was unable to deal with the quick bursts Johnny demanded in the five-a-sides.

Chapter Thirteen

Some Dodgy 'Coaching'

I could have written a small book on our coach journeys alone. It's not that we weren't organised. We always did everything we could to make sure things ran smoothly. But even the most detailed plans have a habit of unravelling at times. One driver had a row with his missus and threw his phone out of the window. Others would turn up and startle us by asking the way. In recent years, just after Gary Megson's departure, one of them, Derek, took a wrong turn coming back from Southampton and the fitness coach Adie Stovell had a pop at him. Derek pulled the bus into the side of the road so he could have a proper go back. There was some grappling and spraying of water before Derek chucked the keys down the coach and told Adie to drive. Rob Hulse stood up for Derek and we eventually calmed things down, the journey continuing when Darren Moore helped get us back on course. He used to play for Portsmouth and knew the area.

Not that local knowledge is always a benefit. Ron Atkinson led us on a short cut round Oxford once and we encountered a bridge so low that one of our party had to stick his head carefully out of the skylight to make sure we were ok. We inched under and were met by a line of cars the other side. The driver of the first one said: "The next bridge is even lower," so it was time to let the suspension and tyres down. We had a double-decker bus for a while, with all the players upstairs and the directors at the back downstairs. The music was blaring out for the entertainment of the squad and there was some forthright discussion as to whether it should stay on – and whether it was possible just to have it heard upstairs. The driver said: "We can't isolate areas. It's either on or off." So one of the directors pulled the wires out.

That particular vehicle provided a challenge when it came to one of my chores. I used to make drinks for the players on board and going upstairs with the teas and coffees was no easy task unless we were cruising on the motorway. Occasionally, I threw a moody and refused to make them if I thought other candidates for the job were hiding behind their lap-tops and not pulling their weight. Coming back from Fulham a few years ago, I suggested someone else should get off their arse and make it. I let it be known that that was me done for the season. Tony Mowbray, as ever, was supportive and said he didn't blame me. When Denis Smith was manager, the coach wouldn't even start when we set off from a hotel just outside Ipswich and the players had to be taken to Portman Road in a fleet of taxis and travel back to the Midlands on the home team's coach.

Things seemed to happen for some reason on trips to Southampton. We had problems with the coach's suspension on the way there for a game in 1985-86 and eventually it went completely, causing us to have a replacement for the journey back. Not that Ally Robertson, Derek Statham and Tony Godden were around to test it out. They shelled out and flew home, although the date of the entry in my diary tells me it was probably more because of their social lives than any concern about the vehicle. It was New Year weekend. It was another trip to The Dell that emphasised what a proud man Johnny Giles is. We got fobbed off with a substitute coach which we didn't like and he said: "We're not turning up at the ground in this." So we arranged for Southampton to send their bus out to us and we dismissed the driver by saying (in other words, lying) that we had more people to take back with us than he had room for, so he could go straightaway. We borrowed the Saints coach and who should we see broken down on the way home but our original one? And, no, we didn't stop to help him out.

Not long after that, we were sharing a vehicle with Wolves – an arrangement that worked okay as Albion's journeys tended to fall when our neighbours were at home, and vice versa. Both of us had FA Cup replays in the same week in 1978-79, though, so they had priority as they had been with the company longer. We ended up on a right charabanc and picked up one of the journalists, the Daily Express's Joe Melling, at the services on the way down. He turned his nose up when he noticed the unfamiliar fixtures and fittings, and was warned "Don't say a word" before being told to draw his curtain. We were ashamed to be seen on that thing.

Other venues brought problems as well. For a Full Members Cup game at Millwall in 1986-87, the directors got in a tizz after they left their coats on board while they were having their pre-match meal. I was under orders to hand them over to them while they were finishing their dessert at the hotel but ran out of time because we were late and I needed to be at the ground to get the kit out and ensure we avoided a fine. It was a difficult trip one way and another and at one point we had to reverse out of a street that was too narrow for the coach. The travelling board members nevertheless took a dim view of being under-dressed on their arrival at the ground and banned me from travelling to the next three away games. Some punishment! I thoroughly enjoyed some Saturdays off with the wife.

I once had to have a lift in a police van to take the kit to Portsmouth because parked cars meant the coach couldn't complete the last 200 yards to Fratton Park. The players had to walk it alongside the fans, as they did at Fulham once. Another famous time the squad got up close and personal with the paying spectators was when Bobby Gould had them setting off on foot to the ground from the hotel where we'd had the pre-match meal at Shrewsbury. He thought it would do them good to feel what the fans were thinking. What our supporters were actually thinking was how good life might be without Bobby because that was the afternoon they were carrying coffins depicting the anticipated end of his reign. Sure enough, it was his last match with us.

Can you believe I drove the bus once to a game? We were just about to set off for Luton when we realised, thanks to all the directors who wanted to travel, that there were more passengers than seats. Ron Saunders, whose relationship with the board was already frosty, was absolutely fuming and saw his chance to make a point. He said: "Right, you, you and you, come in my car. Keith (Leonard), you get yours and take those four. Dave, get the minibus." So I came to drive the squad – or at least a good number of them – to Kenilworth Road for a First Division fixture, no less, on April Fool's Day. Nobby was on board and couldn't believe it. "What's all this about?" he asked. We lost 3-0. It was one of those occasions when those around me realised I could be trusted to toe the club line. One or two of the local press chaps were on to the story and were milling round next day trying to check it out but found me totally unwilling to comment.

There was obviously a good social side to being a board member. The club once took a coach with the directors and their wives to a Cup final and Alan Everiss asked me to go with them to serve the drinks. I didn't fancy it but Mick the driver encouraged me because I would be company for him. We stopped for a meal at The Hilton at Stratford on the way back and Alan slipped us a few quid. Another time, we had a nightmare on the other side of London when I went ahead with the driver and put the kit out for an evening match at Crystal Palace, with the squad still at the hotel. Then it snowed heavily and the game was called off. The players were furious that we had to travel from the centre of London to Selhurst Park to reload the skips before heading home. For a trip to Grimsby once, there was a booking cock-up and we somehow ended up stopping closer to West Brom than Humberside. We were only an hour or so into the trip when the driver caused a few bemused faces on board by pulling in. Apparently, there is a Belton just off the motorway in North Lincolnshire and another one near Grantham. We went for the wrong one and what should have been a 40-minute tootle to Blundell Park on match-day morning turned instead into a trek of an hour and a half. That might have been the trip on which the onward journey was very winding. There was certainly one place we stayed at right out in the country which left us threading our way along the scenic route. There were so many twists and turns that one or two players had to come and sit near the front because they felt sick. There have been better preparations.......

Used right, the team bus is a great place for bonding. Partner whist was the most popular card game for passing the motorway hours for a while and Jeff Astle and Bomber Brown against George Wright and me was a typical 'school'. There was a lot of jiggery pokery over what to lead with and our opponents had it down to a fine art. They would touch the finger to (illegally) tell their partner they were well stocked with diamonds. If they had loads of hearts, they would rub their chest discreetly and would tap their head to denote clubs. To show they had mainly spades, they would somehow try to bend down on the sly. They knew we knew. They would be both at it, with Jeff as the ringleader. The days of such down-to-earth fun on the coach are long gone. Players have lap-tops and computer games now and things are much quieter, except when a big cheer breaks out if someone is forced off the track in one of those formula one races. They all watch their own films, although we have a TV with Sky on it. We have lost something in terms of team spirit with the end of card games.

Graham Roberts and Colin West would play for decent money – the manager would urge them to be sensible but occasionally it got out of hand and someone would blow his win bonus before he had won it. The staff would turn a blind eye. The big bath was another important focal point. What a great place it was to dissect a match you've lost or celebrate one you've won. The room would be full of banter. Now, players disappear quickly to fetch their wives and kids from the players' lounge. I don't think there was a players' lounge until Big Ron's first time here when the lads used a room at the Park Inn, or the Europa as it was first known.

There didn't have to be a team bus for things to go wrong on the road. Nobby Stiles broke down on the M6 once and Roy Horobin had to go to fetch him so he could complete his journey in. And Bill Whitehouse, an odd-job man, managed to knock some double doors out in the Rainbow Stand when he was parking his car. Carlton Palmer – yes, him again! – succeeded in reversing into my car after a home game with Brighton in February, 1987, and breaking my rear lights. There were only two cars on it…..mine and his. And they were 50 yards apart. However did I cope with it all? I became used to problems of all kind. My diary entry for Monday, May 5, 1986, talks of a match between Ron Saunders' first team and the 1978 team, including Laurie Cunningham, for Tony Godden's testimonial, and reveals a certain amount of chaos. "It's the usual behind-the-scenes cock-up; no-one in the office, no-one to open the executive boxes, no Tannoy." It was a sure sign that we weren't the club we had been.

Nobby Stiles was a lovely guy but was very much the in-between guy for a few months of our disastrous relegation season of 1985-86. When he took over from Johnny Giles, he inherited an unwanted fixture from him as well as a plummeting team. It was a friendly at Oldham on their Astroturf and had maybe been agreed by Gilesy as a way of going back to the scene of one of our happiest days together. Unlike the promotion celebrations in the sunshine on April 24, 1976, though, this was a dark, mid-winter night, with hardly anyone there when we arrived. "What the fuckin' hell are we doing here?" Nobby raged. "When I see our John, I'm going to have his guts for garters." It was Valentine's Day night and we were massacred 5-1.

Ron Saunders was the replacement later that month and I knew the players were going to have a tough time with him. One of the first tasks he had me doing was showing him around while he chose a steep hill for fitness training. If there was one player who wasn't going to get on with this Sergeant Major style of management, it was Mickey Thomas. One of the more bewildering conversations I had at the time was when Mickey had an offer to go to America – if I remember right, it was £40,000 for eight months, plus a signing-on fee of £20,000 and an apartment and car – and he still asked me: "Should I take it?" Why the hesitation? I liked Mickey. He was one of the loveable rogues we've had down the years. In my wallet at one point was a cheque he had received from Albion as his signing-on fee. He didn't want it going straight into his bank because his agent would see it and he was due some of it.

I felt an outsider during the Saunders era. He brought in his cronies, like his assistant Keith Leonard (who I mistakenly called Gary after an apprentice we'd had), Norman Bodell (scout/coach) and physio Graham Doig, all from Birmingham, and I struggled to feel part of it. Whether it was through being excluded from meetings or not being told things, I wondered whether I wanted all this and worried that Ron may try to force me out. But I had seen enough comings and goings over the years to know I would probably out-last him. There was nevertheless some pain in the meantime. He casually told me he had sacked Roy Horobin as scout and asked if I knew where Bomber Brown – by now part of our backroom team – lived. That set alarm bells ringing with me for Tony's position. Bomber hadn't heard about Roy's sacking but soon caught up with what was happening. Ron told him to pack his bags as well and he was gone by the same lunchtime. I'd spent 14 years working with Roy, who was a steady enough winger in the late 1950s and a nice man. I'd had more than 20 years with Bomber. Albert McPherson and Ken Hodgkisson had gone in the previous year or two, so I was feeling low. Nobby noticed my mood and I said: "I'm ok. I'll bounce back." But it takes it out of you when you have to wave your colleagues goodbye. Roy was in our Littlewoods syndicate and, after chucking into his leaving collection, I asked him if he wanted one more go, so we might just win and be able to tell the club to stick it.

It didn't end there. George Wright had a row with Ron at the hill and handed in his notice. He went there and then. He had been there for 15 years apart from a spell in Canada with Johnny Giles. He didn't even serve his notice because Ron wanted shut. Norman, who, unlike the others, stayed for a good time, had to look after the injured players for a while. It wasn't long before

Saunders and me had words of our own. I went to tell him my holidays were overlapping with the start of pre-season because I was caught out by the players being told to report back earlier than usual. I said I was sorry and he replied: "I should hope you are. Otherwise, there will be no job for you to come back to." Nobody blamed Saunders for taking us down, though. The season had gone much too far by the time he arrived and things actually improved for me in the early days in the Second Division. I learned he enjoyed a brandy in his room on an overnight trip, so I pulled out the bottle I'd packed in the skip and mixed it with some cokes on the eve of the game at Hull on the first day of 1986-87. The cube I dropped in his glass in room 105 of the Crest Hotel at Ferraby wasn't the only ice broken that night. He took some interest in me and was surprised to learn I had been at the club for 25 years. We were also shocked to discover we had the same birthday (November 6); something we also had in common with Johnny Giles. Friday nights on the road were just about the only time I felt part of it.

I was taken aback when Ron told me before the game against Sheffield United two days later that he was bringing Andy Thompson and Robbie Dennison into the side. I wondered whether he was testing me out to see whether I could keep a secret. He needn't have worried. I knew how to keep mum. The United game was played in some of the worst conditions I can remember as we experienced the tail end of a hurricane raging in the USA. United asked if they could borrow some towels because their dug-out was soaked. We later discovered they had packed them in their skip at the end and they were making off with them when one of the stewards was able to retrieve them. It makes you wonder whether you should bother helping people.

Ron had a difficult job. The fans were against him because of his playing style – and the fact he had managed the Villa and Blues didn't help him here. He had to get some senior players out and the ones he brought in weren't good enough. One of the things he did in his first summer with us was let Alistair Robertson go. He also transported Jimmy Nicholl north to make sure his move to Rangers went through and came back with Bobby Williamson in exchange. When Liverpool came in for Derek Statham, I asked him: "Are you going – or asking for time to think about it?" He laughed. As we both well knew, stepping from the poverty of The Hawthorns to the glitz of Anfield would have had anyone leaping into their car in a flash but injury unfortunately scuppered the deal. Or was it the fact we couldn't find Derek's medical records amid the chaos the place had come to represent?

One deal that rankled big-time was the sale of Steve Bull. Nobby reckoned at the time that Bully, who once scored five in a pre-season win at Stoke, would make it and thought he should be partnered up front with George Reilly. The story was that his first touch was poor, though, and he was sold to Wolves on the same day as Andy Thompson. Over the years, it became more and more obvious to everyone it was a big error. The fans were hurt by the gloating of Wolves supporters as their side came up from the Fourth Division and overtook us. The board here didn't even have the consolation of the sell-on money that would have been due if Bully, who was worth millions in his prime, had moved on again. His captain at Molineux for the first few years at least was none other than Ally Robertson.

As results worsened and loyal servants departed, gallows humour was part of our every-day lives. It got us through. When 40 Russians came to a game, I said: "They are criminals and Siberia wasn't considered to be enough of a punishment for them, so they have been made to come and watch a West Brom home game." Presumably they would have approved of our second strip, which had been changed to all red. I know that had been familiar in the 1960s but this version didn't look like an Albion kit. Doing away with the yellow and green was against Sid Lucas's wishes and it seemed strange because they were the colours Ron was familiar with from his time at Norwich. We introduced blue shorts with the home strip for the first time as well and David Burrows was one of the apprentices asked to come in and pose as a model while the choices were made. My mum did a lot of the patching and stitching, or with numbers that needed sewing on. It was another sign that we were having to be frugal.

We were really on our uppers, with Spring Road – our training base for as long as I could remember – lined up to be sold. When I was asked to work one Sunday because The Hawthorns was being used to stage the Telford v Leeds FA Cup game in the snow, I had to struggle like crazy to get my £22.50 overtime. Poor Kevin Steggles would have sympathised with me. He was put up in a b & b when we signed him on loan. Ron asked Sid Lucas to finance some rugs for the dug-out and his request fell on deaf ears. Sid went as far as urging me to use the tie-ups again and again and, although his heart was in the right place, he was on a real economy drive. He once suggested everyone went to the toilet before arriving at work to save on toilet rolls. Fans might have been very critical of Ron Saunders but they should bear in mind how skint we were.

Ron certainly didn't set out to make friends. He used to have the reserves and apprentices in for training, hard training, on the afternoon of a home night game. He worked all the players harder than they were used to and no session would start without him. Keith Leonard would sit and wait for him, often serving him his coffee first thing in the morning – with two heaped spoonfuls of granules and made with half water and half milk. Once, Mike from accounts said the secretary John Westmancoat was having a half day off but Ron said he couldn't because a player was being signed. I suspect it was Ron being awkward. There was always some friction between him and the directors as well, yet he clung to his luxuries. He always insisted some cigars were packed for him on the trips. But happiness was certainly not a club called West Bromwich Albion........

Chapter Fourteen

One Man Went To Mow

Iknew two of the directors wanted Ron Saunders out and, when Ron Atkinson turned up at Oldham in March, 1987, on the day Don Goodman made his debut, it made me wonder whether they intended to get him back in. A week later, Mick Brown and Brian Whitehouse were at the home game against Sunderland and saw for themselves the mess we were in. My diary reads: "A crowd of barely 6,000 sang repeatedly about us going down and chanted 'Saunders out' and 'Sack the board'. They were gloomy days. The biggest attendance at our ground that season was just under 16,000 for the FA Trophy final replay between Kidderminster and Burton and, for the first time in more than 75 years, our average home crowd was below 10,000.

It was early in the 1987-88 season that Big Ron eventually returned after we had failed to win any of our first six matches and had gone out of the Littlewoods Cup as well. He didn't have much to work with. The quality had gone. He could still get a decent level of performance out of the players but even that wasn't good enough. He was frustrated with the lack of ability. He was helped in his first game, though, when Shrewsbury's Nigel Pearson scored an own goal from 40 yards. In the return at the Gay Meadow in the New Year, Colin Anderson scored the only goal and Sid Lucas couldn't bear to watch the last few minutes. Another relegation battle was looming and he disappeared up the tunnel. Tony Morley kidded him for ages afterwards that Shrewsbury had equalised right at the end. Sid suffered at such times because he was a fan who became chairman. Before he joined the board, he used to be left tickets for games by my first boss Harry Ashley.

Sid's nervousness was justified. We stayed up by a point. There was some good business done, though, with the signings of Brian Talbot and the excellent

105

Chris Whyte. For a week, Ron had done nothing with a letter Chris had sent asking for a trial. Then he acted, had him up for a week and quickly realised he was better than we had. Ron tells me he cost £52,000 for two years and he had a bit of a battle in persuading the board to do it because he hadn't included the PAYE element in his costings to the directors. It was just as well he got his way. As well as playing nearly 100 games for us, Chris made the club money when he was sold to Leeds and became a title winner there. Ron also recalls with some humour the £100,000 signing of Stacey North on the recommendation of the scout Norman Bodell. Apparently, Stacey's partner was present for the talks and chirped up half-way through: "He hasn't half got a good long throw, you know." And he had.

I was more than a kit-man to Ron. I was closer to him than other Albion managers because I saw him away from the club as well. I knew him with his slippers and mug of tea – sometimes in the company of his dad, who also knew his football. The reason for the familiarity was that I cut Ron's lawns in his second spell here. It wasn't my way of creeping to the boss. I got paid for it. He used to love the stripes I put in his garden and could only have been happier if I'd made them blue and white ones. Ron has lived for years in Barnt Green and had Bert Millichip, Ossie Ardiles, Andy Gray, Dean Kiely and Geoff Thomas as near neighbours at various times. Previously, he lived Sutton way and I remember running some bits and pieces to him over there, so I was obviously a bit of a gofer to him for ages.

His lawns must have amounted to around half the size of the Hawthorns pitch, so it wasn't a five-minute job. It meant at least a couple of visits a week in the growing season and my dad would sometimes go as well and tidy up the drive. I couldn't do it all in one day. Ron bought me a sit-on mower eventually. Unfortunately, it was around the time there were a lot of hospital visits with Dad, who died at the age of 89 in 1999. By coincidence and for various reasons, I had to quit with Ron in the same week that he parted with his chauffeur and his partner Maggie lost her cleaner. He told me I could be his driver. He also offered me the kit-man's job when he was at Sheffield Wednesday in the early 1990s and told me not to worry about getting in later than I would be at Albion. I declined and the former Wednesday and Ipswich player Steve McCall did it for a while instead. It just wasn't practical for me, especially with Alison and Clare at school. Apparently, at Manchester United, Ron used to threaten

Norman Davies that he'd fire him and 'get a proper kit-man in.' Norman did almost 25 years' service at Old Trafford before passing away in 2010.

The girls loved Ron being at Albion because they thought the world of his dogs. He and Maggie had four over the years, as I recall......Rambo, Belle, Bambi and Bo. Rambo was the one they remember best and they used to go and play with him at the training ground if they were off school. He was much smaller and cuter than he sounds; certainly nothing like as macho as you'd expect for Big Ron. He would leave them sitting on the chair in the laundry and, thankfully, they were like the players – well trained! There were never any mishaps around the place. Mo, our lovely laundry lady, still talks fondly of Rambo and was much more afraid of Ron than any of his dogs. He scared her to death because he was so big and imposing. He did have a huge persona and presence.

We had Ron's car on the drive at home once while he was in Spain because I was due to take Maggie down to Heathrow, so she could fly out to join him. One Saturday night, we went to the Queens in Halesowen and travelled in style in their Merc. I sat by the window keeping an eye on it. Carol would come on the airport runs as well and we'd go and have a coffee with Maggie before she went through passport control. We saw well beyond his so-called champagne image. He was brilliant at milking an occasion but just loved being surrounded by football people and talking about the game. He was great for the press and entertained them for ages in his office, so they were good to him in return. It didn't work out the second time for him here but he was the most magnetic Albion manager I've known and, in the late 1970s, he gave us the best team in my 50 years at the club. I have a lot to thank him for.

Managers continued to come and go as the club tried to apply the brakes on the slide. In the 1980s, we had reappointed three of our former bosses and then we made Brian Talbot our second player-manager when he took over from Big Ron. After that came a caretaker stint with Stuart Pearson before Bobby Gould also returned to The Hawthorns, where his first spell had been as a player. It was a tough time but not without the occasional laughs. Stuart was once led off by the police for non-payment of fines. It was a set-up by the lads, which the police went along with until they got round the corner. They were supposedly on the way to the station with him on a day we were departing for an away game, if I remember right. The directors were in on it as well.

Carlton Palmer was an entertaining sideshow for much of this time. Things were embarrassing enough when we went to Dumbarton for a centenary match before the 1988-89 season and had a pennant made on which we spelled their name as Dunbarton. Our unease at the reception grew because Carlton and others just wanted to get out for another beer. He had become another victim of the dressing-room pranksters after a game at Stoke in September, 1986, when he scored his first goal in the first team and wouldn't shut up about it. Eventually, a plan just had to be hatched. Derek Statham nipped out and asked one of the office staff, Janet, to type a message telling Carlton to ring Gary Newbon as soon as possible after training so he could be interviewed about his first goal. He duly did and the other lads made sure they were around to hear the call. It went a treat – better than we hoped. Derek joined in and said he had rung Carlton to tell him he had been picked for England under-21s. Carlton's fists and arms were flailing. He was delighted and the lads were congratulating him. He was going home at lunchtime to tell his mom and dad. I can't remember who had to break the news to him that it was a hoax but I hope it was someone who could run.

Carlton's trouble was that he became carried away so quickly. Getting into the first team had gone to his head and he was soon expressing unhappiness about his contract situation and asking Mickey Thomas for John Hollins' phone number. Nobby Stiles had been round the block plenty and advised him to calm down and sign what was on offer at Albion because the money would come in time and he shouldn't be too greedy. Sure enough, he had a terrific career and went on to win the League Cup with Big Ron at Sheffield Wednesday as well as play for Leeds and 18 times for England. It was nice to see a lad from Rowley Regis go on to reach those heights. He had a good role model in Brian Talbot, who picked my brains like no other manager. He presumably thought it was a sign of weakness to go to his coaches, like Big Sam Allardyce, with too many questions. He used to say: "What did so and so do if…..?" I didn't mind telling him. I was glad to help, especially a decent bloke like him who was trying to make his way in management. He got us to the top of the Second Division in the middle of 1988-89 and there was a reminder of the big time when we had a couple of FA Cup ties against Everton. But we couldn't keep it going and tailed off to miss even the play-offs. The number of players he used in his couple of years in charge showed we were still striving to get on top of things. Eventually, it was the FA Cup that did for him when we were humbled at home to Woking.

Just as Ron Saunders left us with something to be grateful for in the form of Don Goodman, so Bobby Gould made one brilliant signing amid a lot of questionable ones. Welcome Bob Taylor. Being relegated to the Third Division at Twerton Park thanks to a draw against one of Bobby's former clubs, Bristol Rovers, was one of the low points of my 51 years at Albion. It was unthinkable considering we had finished fourth in the top flight and qualified for Europe ten years earlier. SuperBob arrived while we were pushing to come back at the first attempt and looked a class act but the atmosphere was often fraught. Bobby started to allow the press into the dressing rooms on a Friday and after a match. It was as if he was fed up of making excuses for the players and thought they should explain themselves. A few weeks after that unusual course of action started, he went a step further and let some supporters in to have their say after a defeat at Bournemouth.

Obviously, at Wimbledon, his squad had reacted right to methods like this and there was another link to his Crazy Gang days after I dropped my guard for a change. I've always been careful not to impose my opinion on a manager unless he has asked for it and think Gouldy seized on a chance this once for a good laugh in the dressing room at my expense. I told him the players were all talk, no action and Bobby relayed it to them. Next day, I was called into the dressing room and the lads were in there. I think it was the big four – Graham Roberts, Paul Williams, Stuart Naylor and Colin West – who took control and had me in the plunge pool fully clothed in no time. I didn't even have chance to take my watch off and put my money safe. It was Bobby's idea of lightening the mood. I thought I was going in again another time, so I had some of their clothes hidden under my tracksuit in case. They spotted what I'd done. It was about the time I got hit on the head with a golf ball by Don Goodman when they were having a chipping competition in the dressing room and I just appeared round the door at the wrong moment. We obviously were a sort of Crazy Gang.

As well as introducing that red and yellow 'Roy of the Rovers' striped change kit, Gouldy had us staying in stately home type places on occasions and there was one hotel that was so out of the way that we had to go down a narrow country line and we were brushing up against the bushes on both sides and scratching the coach. He would be the first to admit he wasn't a success as Albion manager but it's hard not to like him. He came back to The Hawthorns to promote his autobiography to the Supporters Club members two or three years ago and I sat in the audience and bought a copy. He owned up to his mistakes, apologised for where he messed up and was great fun. The fans really seemed to appreciate his honesty. There was one time in the early 1990s when Maureen the laundry lady and me were invited into Bobby's office and he laid on sandwiches and a cuppa. "Stay here for an hour, let the players wonder where you are and let them shout for you," he said. It was to teach them a bit of responsibility and to force them to do something for themselves without being so reliant on us. But it came at a cost. We had to make up that hour at the end of the day to get our chores finished. There was also a tub that they had to throw their wet, dirty kit into but they used to leave it on the floor. Gouldy ordered me one day to leave it and lock up, so they would have to wear it the next day. Apparently, his former chairman had once hosed down the players' kit when they left it strewn around and they had to wear it wet next day. That was presumably Sam Hammam at Wimbledon.

I had something else to thank Gouldy for. He put me and four others, including Mo, on a win bonus. He looked after his staff. He said Mo and me were the best pros at the club. She's a widow and has been there over 30 years. She goes in now by taxi to help out. The bonus idea was Bobby's way of squaring up the earnings a bit because, if you're a fan, as I am, you can be taken advantage of. The arrangement meant I did some catching up because we were in the doldrums in the third tier and it lasted until John Wile was chief executive. I was talked out of it when they offered me a higher basic wage. Unbeknown to me, and due to a clerical oversight, my wages slipped back later towards what they had been. It took me two years to realise. I claimed it back after a bit of a battle and then forgot to ask for the interest. Money wasn't much of a motivation to me, as long as we had enough to live on.

Chapter Fifteen

Welcome, Ossie Mark Two

I was probably too long in the tooth to be excited but I was optimistic and intrigued when we appointed our first foreign manager. Under 1978 World Cup winner Ossie Ardiles, who soon had the lads marvelling at his fantastic touch in training, we were obviously going to attack and play attractive football. By way of keeping the opposition out, he basically used two central defenders and a keeper. The full-backs bombed on all the time, as shown by Nicky Reid scoring in the play-off final at Wembley. Ossie didn't spend much time doing defensive drills. We scored three or more goals in over a dozen home games in 1992-93, including eight against Aylesbury in the FA Cup. His philosophy was just to attack and, if the opposition scored two, we'd score three. To go with Bob Taylor, Ossie signed Andy Hunt in the New Year and it was all a breath of fresh air after the stresses of relegation, something totally different. The players just relaxed a bit and off we went.

Rumour was that Ossie had still been getting paid by his previous club Newcastle, so no wonder he was chirpy. Ronnie Allen used to come in and help and there was always a pot of tea and biscuits before training, which was then at the M & B ground in Smethwick. They had a tea room there and, if we had won on the Saturday, it was chocolate biscuits. Otherwise, they were plain. That was Ossie's idea. We won a lot more than we lost, so we probably all put a few pounds on that season. M & B supplied the beer for the players' bar, which was another popular move. Ossie's assistant, Keith Burkinshaw, was the old school one of the partnership and would be pointing at his watch when training was due to start. He used to say it was half past ten and Ossie would reply: "Relax, we haven't finished refreshments yet." It didn't matter to him whether we started at half past or quarter to. Ossie would turn a blind eye if someone was late in but there's a line and players will take liberties and step over it from time to time. Johnny Giles knew when to go bump and pull them in line. Ossie let it drift.

Another little battle the former Tottenham duo had was over kit. I hated the bar code design shirt. I couldn't stand it at any price (pun intended). Ossie liked baggy shorts down to the knee and Keith wanted them much shorter, if not quite as revealing as they had been in the Ardiles-Hoddle era at White Hart Lane. We had two sets made and Keith won that one. I told him it was the only fight with Ossie he won at Albion. On the training pitch, Keith's was the voice that was heard. Ossie was quietly spoken, so even a rant from him wasn't that daunting. He just went a little more squeaky when he was angry. Coming from Argentina, he had different terminology and you had to listen to him carefully to understand him because he spoke quickly. He certainly wasn't a Martin Jol when it came to the mastery of English. Most of the time, he got by from the touchline by urging the lads to 'Play, play, play.' He was like Johnny Giles in that way. He didn't want anyone to be afraid of receiving the ball. The players loved it and the side clicked. Bob Taylor was up in the mid-30s – that was his goal total, not his age – and we were pushing hard for promotion all season.

We fell five points short of going straight up but came back from a difficult position against Swansea in the play-off semi-final by turning it round on a brilliant night at The Hawthorns. The atmosphere was something else. The club hadn't been to Wembley for 23 years and I was thrilled by the prospect of going there 'hands on' for the first time. I was disappointed for our coach driver Mick Howell that he wouldn't have the same wish fulfilled. He was an Albion fan and would have loved driving the team up Wembley Way. Unfortunately, he had the tricky task a few weeks earlier of telling the chairman Trevor Summers that he would not be driving the squad off on one particular trip until an outstanding invoice from his company, Flights, had been paid by the club. Poor Mick was only the messenger but didn't drive the coach again. Summers kicked him off the job but Mick's devastation was eased by the fact he drove some members of staff and players' wives to Wembley. He appeared in the dressing room after the match when I was in the bath, so we had a chat and commented on the England crest on the tiles behind me.

We had some special shirts made in our yellow and green change colours after our opponents Port Vale had won the toss to wear their first-choice kit and I went early to lay the strips out at Wembley. Enthusiastic tourist that I am, I had my photo taken in the Royal Box by the replacement driver. I had packed a largely unseen but important item in the skip – Popeye the lucky mascot. It was a doll belonging to an Albion fanatic called Bill Martin, who came to games and training on his bike. He received no pay but helped out by retrieving the balls from down the bank when we had trained at Spring Road. He worked out in the gym, didn't have an ounce of fat on him and loved developing his muscles. Hence his nickname Popeye. He was in his late 60s or even his 70s and lived in a flat on his own in Smethwick. A succession of managers, including Ossie, took to him and Andy Gray made a particular fuss of him. Ron Atkinson even played him in an eight-a-side game after telling George Reilly to clear off because he was always injured. The Popeye mascot lived in the skip for years but I made sure I took it out at Wembley and Ossie had it by him. You can see him holding it up on the after-match photos.

Bill had a knack of always getting from A to B. John Reynolds from the accounts department was supposed to bring him back from Swansea but there was no sign of him and, while I was loading the coach up, a search of all the toilets took place in case Bill had collapsed. They eventually assumed he had arranged an alternative lift – and he had. He was back at The Hawthorns long before any of us. Another time, he wanted desperately to go to a reserve game at Manchester United or Liverpool and sneaked on the coach. The players thought it was a big joke and said nothing as he hid at the back. Stuart Pearson rumbled him later, though, and kicked him off. I hope it was at least at the services. Stuart was not one of his admirers. Tragically, Bill died after being knocked off his bike near Rolfe Street and had a big turn-out from the club, including players, at his funeral.

I had Status Quo blaring out on the coach on the way to Wembley. It was absolutely rocking. We really were up for that game, or most of us were. My assistant Barry Wyle was so nervous beforehand that he was in the first aid room being calmed down. He was a big fan. Vale had finished four points ahead of us and beaten us home and away but we were always in control, although we had to wait until the second half – and after they had been reduced to ten men by Peter Swan's sending-off – to score our three goals. Keith Burkinshaw said the support we had that day was the best he had ever known. The lads gave them plenty to sing about and the celebrations afterwards were something else. I felt like a bit of a spare part but Gary Robson and Gary Strodder each grabbed one of my arms and made sure I was on the celebration photo by saying: "Come on, you're part of the team." It was my first time on the Wembley pitch. Next thing I know, Barry is on the picture as well. He was lying on the driver's bunk on the way home, an emotional wreck!

There was no big do afterwards in London – maybe we couldn't afford one. We all went back to the ground and were in the room on the Halfords Lane side where the museum used to be. No-one seemed to know what to do with the winners' trophy, so I took it home for the evening and had a few photos taken with it in the company of Carol and the girls, who had thoroughly enjoyed their own day out at Wembley with the supporters. Alison had gone with her mum on a coach containing various members of club staff while Clare went by car with her boyfriend at the time and now partner again, Charlie Hurst, and his brother Bradley. They are sons of one of our directors, Barry Hurst. Round about that time, Clare and Charlie worked part-time together in the club shop, which no doubt did good business at what is regarded as the start of our boing-boing era. I had a little business of my own to attend to the day after Wembley. The wooden base had broken on the lap of honour, which I was flattered to be part of, so I administered a little DIY as best I could.

It had been a super season after the previous three, which had been spent either in what we used to call the Third Division, or trying to stay out of it. It was nice to be a winning team again and I'm sure Ossie enjoyed his red wine by way of celebration. That was his favoured tipple on the overnight stays and I had grown to like his company. Working with him was a great time but, within a month, Spurs had come in for him and he was gone. His good work with us had obviously been noted. I was not surprised he accepted their offer. He was never going to say no to his beloved 'Tottingham'.

A book written by my long-time Spurs counterpart Roy Reyland refers to Ossie's successor Keith Burkinshaw as a dour Yorkshireman, Well, he also had a dry sense of humour. He didn't shout a lot from the dug-out. It was as if he had said what he needed to say before the players went out, tactical adjustments aside, and it was up to them once the game started. He had had nothing like the playing career Ossie had enjoyed. He appeared in just one game for Liverpool before going off to play in the lower divisions and then become a successful manager. He signed Ossie for Spurs and also had a laid-back side to him. He didn't even bother going on one of the Anglo Italian trips in his first few months in charge. He left the job to his assistant Dennis Mortimer when we played in Fiorentina, where Ronnie Allen was among our travelling entourage.

In Keith's first season, we just avoided returning to the level we had worked so hard to escape from the previous spring. As we were inclined to do, we took it to the last day before getting out of jail with Lee Ashcroft's winner at Portsmouth. Then, in 1994-95, we were on the back foot straightaway because of the difficult time we had through starting the season with five successive away League matches. Stadium redevelopment meant we couldn't use The Hawthorns for a First Division game until well into the second month – a sequence that also contained a League Cup trip to Hereford. We lost the second leg of that tie to go out and there was the familiar feeling of the pressure building. We even had an appearance by the chairman Trevor Summers alongside us on the bench for a game at Tranmere. A few of us raised our eyebrows but nothing surprised Keith. "If that's what he wants to do...." he said. We lost 3-1 and Keith was gone soon afterwards, to be replaced by Alan Buckley, who seemed to be in two minds over the ground redevelopments. Extensive work was done at both ends of The Hawthorns to make it all-seater but he thought it was an extravagance and wondered why we needed new offices, which were built 300 yards down Halfords Lane in the Tom Silk Building, along with a new club shop. He would have preferred any spare money going into the team. Mind you, he had known life at Walsall and Grimsby, where facilities were more modest, so you could see his point. And he soon started to stock the squad with players he had known on Humberside. On the other hand, it was our bigger-club feel that attracted him here in the first place. When he came to watch a game just before his appointment, he was in his car as the thousands of fans poured in and he apparently said to his assistant Arthur Mann: "We've got to have a bit of this." We had a particularly big crowd at home to Bristol City a few weeks into his reign when the redeveloped ground was officially opened on Boxing Day.

Some of our back-up facilities still left a bit to be desired. Richard O'Kelly and John Trewick used to go and look at parks, schools and works pitches for the younger players to train on. And they'd put a set of five-a-side goals in the minibus. It was utterly frustrating for the coaching staff. If they wanted to draft a player in from one group to another, it meant sending a car to do it. It's so much better now obviously with a superb training ground. Results were up and down in Alan's first few months but we managed to stay well clear of the sort of nerve-tingling survival battle we had come through by winning at Fratton Park on the last day of the previous season.

Strange things then happened in 1995-96. When we went to Millwall in the last game of October, they were top and we were second. They won 2-1 but ended up going down. Starting that afternoon, we went on a run of 14 defeats in 15 games, with the other – at home to Wolves – drawn 0-0 after Andy Hunt had a penalty saved. We looked like going down as well, then produced a run of form even better than we had started the season with and finished comfortably in mid-table. The difference was Richard Sneekes, who Alan signed from Bolton and who came up with ten goals in no time. He did all right the following season as well, with Alan fortunate to have inherited two very good strikers in Bob Taylor and Andy Hunt. He loved working with them and still liked a game himself. When he played in a testimonial at Villa, he asked me to get him some boots ready and I mischievously cut through the new laces I had placed on the top. He didn't realise until he came to put them on and I can just picture him shouting: "Matthews!" I did put another set inside, though, to see he was all right.

We just seemed stuck in a rut where we changed managers every year or two and Tony Hale and his board had faces like thunder at Molineux after Wolves completed a high-scoring double over us in the New Year. That was Alan's time almost up and the change that inevitably followed saw Ray Harford appointed, with Cyrille Regis as one of his coaches. John Trewick was also part of the senior backroom team and often took training the day before a game because the POETS principle was in place at the time – Piss Off Early, Tomorrow's Saturday. Ray, who would often get back to his home in the south east after doing his morning press conference, wasn't here five minutes, which was a pity. He was nothing like the dour individual some took him for as a result of his TV interviews. He enjoyed mimicking the West Midlands accent by confusing 'cuppa tae' with 'kipper tie' and was always generous if one of his flutters on the horses came good. More than once, he handed Alison £20 out of his winnings and told her to buy cakes for the girls in the office. Ray gave us a brief taste of the top of the table the following autumn but then he walked out, saying he wanted to be closer to his home. He got himself fixed up at QPR.

Events took a sinister twist in the October after the drug testers turned up at the training ground at the university and asked me to come up with three or four numbers in an 'unlucky' dip. I pulled Shane Nicholson's number out of the hat and he had to take a test, which he failed. He had been taking things he shouldn't have and was suspended pending a hearing. He received a ban and was sacked by the club but Chesterfield gave him a chance and there were no hard feelings against me. He might have got into more trouble in the long run if he hadn't been found out when he was. It was still a big story. We'd had the Willie Johnston scandal in 1978 when he was sent home from the World Cup finals in disgrace but that was seen more as a Scotland matter than an Albion one, although the club doctor, Roger Rimmer, was less than impressed at reading reports of how he had supposedly dealt with Willie's hay fever by recommending tablets that were available over the counter at the chemist. Just about the biggest involvement we'd known with the popping of pills before then was that clever ploy Len Cantello, Asa Hartford and others adopted – of taking Ex-Lax before they had to step on the scales. They figured that a couple of hasty trips to the loo wouldn't do them any harm when their weight was checked.

Chapter Sixteen

These Boots Are Made For Working

Players used to throw bouquets of flowers into the crowd when we went abroad to play friendlies. On a pre-season trip somewhere I didn't go, our young full-back Roger Minton was apparently shouting 'woman, woman' as he hurled his on to the terraces because he felt embarrassed at the thought they might be going to a bloke. The players ribbed him rotten. In more recent years, it has been commonplace, against my wishes, for players to lob bits of kit to supporters as souvenirs, especially at the end of a season. Some clubs charge players for the cost of the shirt if they do this and I nagged our lads to hang on to them in case we ran short in the spring. Ben Foster had much better sense of timing. When he threw a load of gloves in among the supporters after a game against Arsenal, it was the last day of the season – also the last match before my retirement and the final one with Roy Hodgson in charge. And the general mood was good because we had done well to pull clear of trouble. Another year, we knew we were struggling because one player chucked his boots to the fans and was miffed to see them land at his feet again. Someone had thrown them back.

Boots were a big part of my working life. The old ones used to go in a big skip and, when Kanu was here, he would send them to Nigeria, preferably signed. His took up more space than most. He was a size 13. At the other end of the scale, Rob Earnshaw's were a five, so I probably popped to the club shop to buy his socks from off the kids' shelf. An alternative for discarding old footwear was to auction it off for charity. One of Jeff Astle's daughters paid about £30 for Ishmael Miller's boots once. I was busy at the start of these items' life as well because ordering footwear for the new intake of apprentices was another of my jobs. Inevitably, they would ask for ones that were too big because they were used to their parents buying them in sizes that meant they could grow into them. But we wanted them in a pair that fitted perfectly without any slack. White boots were a fad for a while in the 1960s and 1970s, especially when Alan Ball and Alan Hinton wore them. Asa Hartford was the first Albion player I can remember painting his and he was soon told to blacken them again. The manager wouldn't have it. Players get very attached to particular boots and there was a time when they would play in them long after they should have been thrown in the rubbish skip rather than the match-day one. Nowadays, if a player has a bad game, he'll have a new pair – and suppliers are only too keen to provide them so they get exposure on TV. All colours do now. We've had Peter Odemwingie in light green and Romelu Lukaku in yellow and orange. Midfielders and strikers tend to go for the fancy colours and defenders are generally more no-nonsense, although Martin Albrechtsen caused a stir when he reported back from one summer in Scandinavia with multi-coloured boots. They were revolutionary at the time, less so now. Steven Reid started 2012-13 in jazzy red.

Another difference is the weight. The boots now are so flimsy you could fold them in half. They are great for packing in the skip but offer next to no protection. I'm convinced that's why there are more injuries, especially to the metatarsals. Who had even heard of those bones before David Beckham and Wayne Rooney broke them? I tried to suggest a happy medium in the dressing room because the manager wants the players content in their own minds but also insists they follow his orders. Gary Megson wouldn't let me pack moulded boots. He thought they were too lightweight and didn't give the same confidence as studs when players went into a tackle. I agreed with him most of the time but used to turn a blind eye and wait to see if Gary, Frank Burrows or Gary Shelton noticed someone breaking ranks. I'd go round the players at half-time anyway and tell them to lift their feet so I could brush the grass or mud off. I was bound to see what they were in. If someone was struggling to keep their footing and I knew why, I might just say 'So and so is slipping over all the time' to bring the gaffer's attention to it. It was telling on them in a way but it was also for their own benefit. They might have been dropped for the next week if they had stayed as they were. Players would moan at me for 'shopping' them but I told them to get on to Gary as it was his idea. Some even smuggled their moulds into games in their toiletries bag.

Blades, so-called because of the blade-shaped rubber or aluminium studs, tend to allow players to glide over grass but Sir Alex Ferguson argued strongly against them. He believes they are prone to causing injury and prefers boots that get a grip on the turf. I prefer a traditional screw-in stud with the length changeable. On a firm but dewy surface, you'd have short studs. On a softer pitch, you'd go for longer. Managers do their nut when players come off and change during games. That's what the warm-up is for. Years ago, on an icy pitch, you would leave the head of the nail protruding for extra grip, although it was an obvious injury risk to the opposition. There was a maximum and minimum permitted length of stud at one point and referees would come in and inspect them. It was a farce because players would have them inspected and then change into another pair at the last moment if they wished. And who checks them now? No-one. Only substitutes have theirs inspected as they go on. The pitches are so good now and so uniform, I can't remember the last time I ordered any studs.

Gary Megson also hated coloured boots. Andy Johnson brought a red pair in once just to wind him up and they soon went missing. Joke or not, he wasn't having them. AJ thought I'd pinched them on the gaffer's orders and swears to this day I did. Perhaps he's not a bad judge. My reply has always been the same: "I couldn't possibly say, Andy. But what do you do if your boss gives you instructions?" Jason Roberts once complained that I wouldn't give him some new bladed boots and I took the brunt, although it was Gary's decision. Gary hated blades and rubber soles as well. Jason already had six pairs but claimed none of them were any good. Players get boots thrown at them now by Nike and other companies because the club are in the Premier League and on TV. Jason should have seen Simeon Hodson's boots when he came from Newport in the 1980s. There were more patches on them than there was original boot.

There were other footwear issues. One Albion player went off to play for England and I had a phone call saying he had no boots. He thought they would be provided. I had to go in on the Sunday and sort them out for someone to drive them down to him, probably at Bisham Abbey. It's nothing now for a player to want six pairs of boots taking to a match. Mickey Thomas would take four and then complain to me that he really wanted a pair I'd left behind. David Mills was one of the first players I remember having inserts added to his footwear because of injury. Boots used to be numbered on the heels so I could spot them when they were in the pigeon holes in the bootroom. Players had training numbers before squad numbers came in and that's how I'd mark them. If a player missed an open goal and was accused of having his boots on the wrong feet, I might mark them 'left' and 'right' for the following game.

We wouldn't put initials on boots because someone from the opposition camp would often come into the dressing room, supposedly to have a word with me. Really, he had been sent on a spying mission by his gaffer and his eyes would be flashing all round the room. This would be more of a danger at an away game, where, from possibly the late 1970s, I would pop to the ground early and put the kit out on the pegs. I know the snooping went on because I did it as well. Before one match at The Hawthorns, I went into the visitors' dressing room on the pretext of seeing what equipment they had to carry their kit in and to ask their kit-man how much they actually laid out for games. I wasn't being too much of a sneak but just happened to notice whose shirts were hanging up and relayed it back to our manager. When the team-sheet came round, it was nothing like the team I had reported back with. I'd been done like a kipper. Ten out of ten for that! I made plans to send out occasional red herrings myself. Names on shirts made this practice more widespread, so, if intruders were likely, I delayed putting shirts out when I could, or turned them round to hide the names.

I would only find out what our line-up was once the manager had told the players at the team meeting. That would be a Saturday lunchtime and I'd hear it first-hand if it was an away game. At home matches, players arrived about an hour and a half before kick-off, so I would phone the physio for news as I didn't go to the team meetings, which have been at the training ground in recent years. I put the wrong kit out once for a 4-0 home win over Stockport. I had Jordao as playing, when he was only sub, and had Warren Cummings on the bench when he had been dropped altogether. The manager wasn't happy. It was New Year's Day and I don't know whether I'd had a bit to drink the night before and wasn't at my sharpest. Well, I'm only human. With Danny Dichio having his car broken into and three of the windows smashed while the game was going on, it was just another day at the madhouse; underlined when I heard Stockport's manager – Carlton Palmer, no less – telling his players he was going to jack it in if they didn't give him more effort.

The dressing room was a place of many moods. Before the match, it would be all about anticipation and excitement. Afterwards, it could be jubilant, content, miserable or angry. If there were bollockings being dished out, it generally held me up. I could hardly go round the players asking for their gear for washing if an irate manager was in full flow. And they would be slower undressing and showering if we had lost – possibly because of the understandable reluctance to rush out to face directors, supporters, pressmen and even family. For decades, there has been a wooden block in the middle of the Hawthorns dressing room which players kick to break in new boots. One manager took a swing at it with his foot after we had conceded a late equaliser and needed treatment from the physio. The first aid kit was needed another time when a furious Alan Buckley pushed the dressing room door open so hard that he cut the head of the physio, who just happened to be standing behind it. I had seen and heard the ranting all before, of course, but had to bide my time with my post-match chores, discreetly picking up a boot here and a pair of shorts there. At calmer times, I would just descend on the players for their discarded kit as they stripped off.

Security was always on my mind. When we moved out of Spring Road for 12 months to train at Aston University, I fetched and carried the kit every day because I was uneasy that the students might find it too much of a temptation. The loss of kit that most sticks in my mind, though, was when Everton were here for the first home game of a season a few years back and we also had carpenters, electricians, plumbers, painters and cleaners around. The stairs were being edged and I don't know how we were given a health and safety certificate. There was wet paint around and the Everton kit-man struggled to navigate a way though all the workmen. It was chaos and a load of shirts and shorts that were going to be worn that day went missing. Fortunately, we had replacements. Security of strips was my responsibility but there were extraordinary circumstances that day with the finishing touches being put to the major redevelopment of the stand. And I was in the staff room at the time putting the coaching team's gear out.

That isn't to say plenty of items didn't go missing at other times. Alan Stephenson from the commercial department and Bobby Gould went bananas once when a set of kit went missing from an embroiderer's just before we were staging our annual photo call on the pitch. And, around the same time, a player was so irritated by a label rubbing his neck that he went to bite a way through it to take it out but put a big hole in the shirt instead. The lads were often seeking whole garments for themselves. Paul Bradshaw used to carry a big bag and went to the laundry once and put some t-shirts, sweaters and rain jackets in it. Maureen the laundry lady tipped me off and, when the players were out training, I emptied the contents. He could hardly complain, could he? Maybe he wanted to do some training at home or he had promised someone a piece of kit. I used to tell the players not to nick anything. I'd help them if I could, even if the answer was often no.

Years later, Darren Bradley volunteered the confession that he had taken some sweaters for his Sunday team without us being any the wiser. They reckoned I was tight with my kit and he had the answer. Twice over, in fact. During the kick-in, he used to deliberately send wayward passes or shots to his mates in the crowd. They would let the balls down and put them in a bag. If we sent ten balls out for the warm-up, it was a regular occurrence that only eight would come back. I had told the stewards to keep an eye open, thinking a spectator was up to no good. You couldn't knock Darren's enterprise. I often came to dread school holidays in other eras because the kids would be waiting on the other side of the fence at the training ground and off they would go with a ball. Some players would probably do it on purpose. The balls cost us £30 and were worth £90. Training now is with an actual match ball.

Disappearance of a more routine kind came while we were training at the M & B ground 20 years or so ago. Players were losing money from their pockets, just a fiver here and a tenner there. The thief was crafty in not emptying their wallets but just getting some beer money for himself and obviously hoping his deeds would go unnoticed. We used to have a cup of tea in the pavilion before training and I'd go back to the ground in the minibus but Norman Bodell waited in the changing room behind the door this one day and the culprit would have assumed everyone was off site. Norman caught him red-handed. It was one of the groundsmen. Less seriously, an Albion pennant went missing in February, 1987. I was getting it signed for a young lad who had sent it in. Carlton Palmer didn't realise he was doing wrong by helping himself to it. I challenged him, got the £2.50 back and bought another one. Steve MacKenzie complimented me on my performance and I said it was no performance. The other lads saw a picture of some prisoners behind bars and super-imposed Carlton's picture on it. He apologised. Players just take an autographed ball or shirt and don't think. It was always something for nothing. They push their luck because they don't think it's your property to lose. If you say no, they don't like you but I felt responsible for the club's money in my department. I was accountable for it. I moaned a couple of years ago at a member of staff who gave a six-pair pack of socks away to a player. These guys can afford 12 packs, no problem.

There might easily have been other stories of woe to tell in this section. I once got my nephew Ivan a bit of work at the club and, as he was sweeping up round the turnstiles, he realised there was a bag of money, containing hundreds of pounds, among all the cigarette boxes and the sweet wrappers. How it got there was never explained. Another time, Mo was cleaning in the ticket office and found bundles of cash in a waste paper basket. Away from the ground, two young keepers were in digs together and one was forging the other's signatures on cheques and helping himself to the contents of his bank account. Credit to the club, they dispensed quickly with his services. And a girl in the ticket office was caught on camera putting money down her bra.

My main problems were making sure I didn't forget anything. So what did I have to transfer from that kit room at the training ground, or tardis or bunker as we sometimes called it, to the skip for our trips? The list of items grew rapidly in later years, with the introduction of more substitutes, more members of backroom staff and more progressive thinking. Not long ago, I found out an old check list, which I'm guessing dated back to the 1970s. It showed what I packed for an away game: 1 set shirts, numbered from 2-12, 2 spares; 1 dozen shorts; 1 dozen socks (stockings as we then called them); 12 jock straps; 12 slips (briefs); 1 goalkeeper shirt; 1 under-shirt; 1 keeper's gloves and cap; 24 towels; boots; rubbers (trainers); 4 tracksuits (for the substitute and coaching staff); 2 sweaters; a trainer's shirt, shorts and socks; 1 trainer's bag. There might also have been a complete second strip – usually a change kit in case of a colour clash. This would all go in a wicker skip that looked like a giant picnic basket.

In recent years, with the volume of gear so much greater, aluminium-type skips have been in fashion and the contents are something like: 40 match shirts with names on (two for each player as they often like a fresh one at half-time, plus spares); 40 match shorts; 40 pairs socks; 40 slips; 4 blood shirts (unnumbered and to be worn if a cut player is ordered by the referee to change); 25 t-shirts and sweat tops (for warming up and, in some cases, for warming down after a game); 20 pairs gloves; hats; 20 undershirts; 20 undershorts (cycling-type); 20 bench coats (one for each of the substitutes plus the backroom staff and the non-playing squad members); boots; trainers; flip-flops; 60 towels (enough for two each for everyone who gets stripped).

Typically, six skips have been needed in the last few seasons, with the match-day entourage stretching beyond coaches and perhaps two physios to masseurs, a doctor and two kit-men. There would also be bags – a huge polythene one in the old days – containing dozens of odds and ends, including laces, tie-ups, studs, spanners, pliers, cotton wool, chewing gum, polish, a stop watch, shin pads, knee pads, safety pins and black armbands. You would have found a gallon jug, bandages, chiropody set, shampoo and soap on the list in decades gone by. Now, the players will take their own toiletries and the physios and doctors will see to the first-aid and medical items. But I had to take extra cotton bandages fora time as Nicky Shorey wanted them for his tie-ups.

My golden rule was never to be short, so we always had a full load on for journeys. I learned that you shouldn't give the players chance to blame anyone else for their performance. And, because I packed as far in advance as I could, I often took a change kit just in case the club decided, as they occasionally did, to play in different colours for commercial reasons, even if there was no clash. There were times, though, when I was caught out. Once, I realised I'd forgotten the players' slips on an overnight trip and asked Alison if she would go and collect them from Maureen as she was travelling to the game on a supporters' coach next day. Well, it was that or dash round Marks and Spencer! Alison found a big black plastic bag for them and met me at the ground to hand them over but insisted we did so outside in case she was searched at the turnstiles and asked to explain why she was carrying 30 odd pairs of men's underpants.

Another time, I forgot that clubs could name more substitutes for the Anglo Italian Cup than in League matches and found myself short. Fortunately, we were only at Birmingham in a preliminary round match rather than somewhere down on the Adriatic, so I sent my assistant, Mark 'Bamber' Gascoigne, back on the team coach to pick up some extras. On other occasions, when I felt the workload demanded it and the club were hesitating over whether to send a second kit-man on overnight trips, I had him sleeping on the sofa of my room.

Players would be measured for shirts and shorts at the start of a season and they would be stuck with that size until the following summer. Some preferred a baggy fit, others something much tighter, so there was always plenty to organise. Some, like Filipe Teixeira if I remember right, liked long sleeves whatever the weather. Darren Moore, on the other hand, would go out in short sleeves even if it was minus four. So much for the old Arsenal system whereby all the players would wear the same......short sleeves early and late season, long for the colder months in between. With all these different items, you can see why a match day was a very full-on experience for me. There was always a player in need of a change of shorts – Len Cantello whipped his torn pair off once in front of a crowd of 53,000 in an FA Cup tie at Everton and pulled a replacement pair on – or new socks. And the lads required any number of replacement items at half-time when the air was full of the smell of sweat, dampness, the leather of the boots and possibly another blast of muscle spray. Before kick-off or after showering, the scent of after shave was the one most likely to greet you.

With me in the dug-out were all the emergency spare items of kit, especially laces, boots, socks and the blood shirts and shorts. There were also replacement studs, even pliers and spare balls in case the match one went down or disappeared into the crowd and one of Darren Bradley's mates got his hands on it! Looking after the kit, Monday to Friday as well as on match days, became a huge job – and not just for me. Mo the laundry lady and her assistant Lyn could get through five boxes of 9,960kg of washing powder a day in the club laundry, which had four industrial-sized washing machines and four big tumble driers. This area of the operation had come a long way since the players had been told by Jimmy Hagan that their training kit had to last for more than just one day. And it probably wasn't that long before then that the match-day kit would have been plonked in the middle of the dressing room in one big bag and the players helped themselves almost on a first-come-first-served basis.

On the team front, we were in a phase of managers coming and going without that much changing. Denis Smith was appointed on Christmas Eve, 1997, so his first or second training session was a 6pm work-out on Christmas Day before we travelled to play at Reading. We lost there but drew with his former club Stoke a couple of days later and then beat them in the FA Cup a couple of weeks later to give him his first win. I told him there was no Cup atmosphere in the squad before we went to Villa in the fourth round. Sure enough, we lost 4-0. We were using the Villa team coach at the time and still had it when we went to Wolves at the end of January. I cut a headline out of the Daily Mail quoting Steve Bull as saying we had no chance in the Black Country derby. I also found one, completely unrelated to football, saying: "You have no bottle." I asked the gaffer if I could post them on the notice board in an effort to provoke the players. Occasionally, you can get a reaction from things like that. Andy Hunt scored our winner at Molineux and the good spirits of the day continued when I slipped and fell over trying to reach a ball.

I had something extra to pack on overnight trips with Denis…..some casual non-Albion clothes. He loved a Friday night in a country pub. He was particularly at home when we went to Oxford and drank at a place in the Cotswolds. If you pardon the pun, he looked very much the Lord of the Manor because he had managed down there. Another time, he had us entertained by Charlie Drake at a hotel on the way to Ipswich or Norwich. A couple of years later, one of the players, Tony Grant, had a fashion matter on his mind as well. He complained that the kit was too big on him and said he was used to a tighter fitting shirt. I convinced him that because we were called the Baggies, ours had to be a bit more baggy. In truth, there was not the special tailoring to suit players' individual needs that there is now.

Despite the arrival of Malcolm Crosby, which improved things for a while, I didn't think the players were really playing for Denis but his reign was a long one compared with that of Brian Little, who was in and out in the space of a season – complete with the motor bike and leathers we had a chuckle at on the occasions when he arrived on two wheels. We were in a mid-table rut but the place was anything but dull after Brian had gone. His replacement was one Gary Megson.

Chapter Seventeen

Heading Upwards With Megson

I didn't like Gary Megson's style of football and remember telling Kanu that he would have to get used to giving a pass and not getting the ball back. I'm an Albion fan and was brought up on the likes of Jimmy Hagan, Alan Ashman and Ron Atkinson; men who believed in an entertaining, attacking style that is in keeping with the club's traditions. Gary had different views – some of them influenced by the limited funds at his disposal – but the players bought into his ways because we quickly became a winning team again. As a Championship club over two or three seasons, if we got our noses in front, we knew we weren't going to lose and would probably win. Whatever I might say about playing styles, Gary was great with me and we have much to thank him for. He led us to the Premier League for the first time and, by then taking us back there, paved the way for the more comfortable times we have had in the top flight in recent years.

Gary's first few months were all about keeping us in the Championship and the fight was won only on another of those tense last days that we became used to before and after the turn of the century. It was us or Walsall to go down but we managed to win our home game against the champions Charlton while the Saddlers lost at Ipswich. The tension was good news for Wrigley's. Gary was on four packets of chewing gum a match at the time – I gave him two before kick-off and two more at half-time. Well, he needed to keep his jaws loose for all that shouting. The following season, from nowhere, we nearly went up. We reached the play-offs and were two up against Bolton in the home leg of the semi-final before being pulled back and then well beaten at their place. He had raised the club's sights and showed his fiery side early the following season when we were signing Darren Moore from Portsmouth. He was not impressed

Manager Ron Wylie holds court during a trip to Barcelona for a pre-season tournament in 1982. Seated in a red bib and facing the camera is Martin Jol while Ally Robertson is on the right in the foreground in the no 10 shirt. The duo are reunited below nearly 25 years later when the Dutchman brought his Tottenham team to The Hawthorns. On the right is Jol's then assistant Chris Hughton.

Left: Celebrating the winning of the Third Division play-off final trophy with my loyal 'work wife' Mo, the club's popular laundry lady. Below: A bit of banter, by the looks of it, with my assistant for several years, Mark 'Bamber' Gascoigne, with Darren Purse also in attendance.

No introductions required......one of my early Albion heroes on a visit back to the ground in recent years. I was hardly going to miss this photo opportunity, was I? I'm sure I got an autograph or two as well. Below: All in the interests of team spirit.....time for a quick 'livener' with masseur Derrick Jones before the players change into their match kit for the Championship play-off final against Derby in 2007. Derrick was a good friend who sadly lost his battle against cancer after I embarked on one of my own. It was a Baggies tradition that I always had a sociable drink with close colleagues before kick-off, with the manager often included.

Above: Shirts, shirts everywhere and very much standing room only for me during one of my frequent check-list sessions. More tools of the trade are on display (left) as a training session allows me something of a breather. Below: A washing line rather than a forward line is the order of the day - the result of a fire in our laundry which led to us and our neighbour Margaret pitching in to help with the effort to get a mountain of kit cleaned and dried in time for match-day.

Above: Presentation time to mark my long service. Brendon Batson is seen holding the Merit Award I received from Premier League sponsors Barclays soon after my 50th anniversary. At the same time, Albion's chief executive Mark Jenkins hands over some cut-glass on behalf of the club. I believe I'm only the second person, other than a player or manager, to receive this recognition from Barclays. Another treasured prize on my CV is the Laraine Astle Award - presented annually in memory of one of my very best Albion pals, Jeff Astle. I was honoured in 2004-05 with that award. Right: A picture with a man who must have a room full of awards at home, Arsenal boss Arsene Wenger.

AF/LL

28 January 2011

Mr D Matthews
Kit Manager
West Bromwich Albion Training Ground
430 Birmingham Road
Walsall
WS5 3LQ

Dear Dave

Many congratulations on reaching such an amazing landmark of 50 years service at West Bromwich Albion. Thinking back and I maybe correct here   that   you   were probably there to welcome a great Scots player Bobby Hope to your Club! Now that is a long time.

Having had two fantastic men as my kit men in Norman Davies who passed away about 5 years ago and now Albert Morgan, I take it you pick the team, wash the kit, drive the players here there and everywhere, act as a confidant to them, protect them from the Manager etc, well that's my experience of those two has been. Oh and by the way you will have better gear from your supplier than everyone else!

Taking all that away I know you have been a great credit to West Bromwich Albion and to Football, it is people like you that reinforces our belief that there are good people in the game so on behalf of everyone here at Old Trafford may I congratulate you on your 50 years service and wish you good health and happiness for the future.

Yours sincerely

Sir Alex Ferguson CBE

MANCHESTER UNITED FOOTBALL CLUB LIMITED
Trafford Training Centre, Birch Road off Isherwood Road, Carrington, Manchester M31 4BH
Telephone: 0161 868 8700. Facsimile: 0161 868 8855. www.manutd.com
Registered in England No. 95489, VAT No. GB 561 0962 51
Registered office: Sir Matt Busby Way, Old Trafford, Manchester M16 0RA

With Alison, Carol and Clare at the dinner the Supporters Club kindly organised in 2011 to mark my 50 years at Albion. Left: a letter of congratulations from Sir Alex Ferguson - part of a bumper collection of tributes from Premier League managers. There was some reluctance among my family for this photo below to be taken as it captures my stay in hospital during my cancer treatment. But I insisted: "Take it. We can use it in the book!"

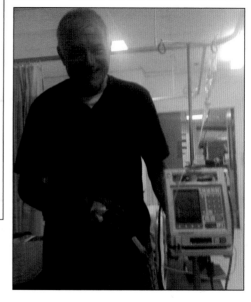

One for the scrapbook......at the dinner to celebrate my 50th anniversary, I had named Roy Hodgson as the best of all the managers I had worked for at the club. Well, he was my boss at the time and he was in the room! I genuinely wish I could have worked with him for longer. I was in the dug-out for one last time for Roy's final game before he took up the England post. Next to me for the day was Joe Bradley, an assistant to my successor Pat Frost. He seems to be finding our defeat by Arsenal too much to bear.

when John Wile said Big Dave was moving house and couldn't meet him for talks. Gary was in a rush to have him in his squad for a Worthington Cup tie at Cambridge.

Life was never dull under Gary's management. He once gave some little footballs away to youngsters sat near the dug-out and another time handed out loads of chewing gum. It was his way of saying sorry for the bad language they sometimes had to put up with from him. He obviously cared because one of the acts of apology came at the same time that his wife had been very ill in hospital. That wasn't his only familiarity with health issues. In a home game against Gillingham early in our first promotion season, he told the players at half-time that Frank Burrows had left the ground early not feeling well. It turned out he had cancer of the kidney. Gary was incredibly passionate about football but these occurrences helped give him a sense of perspective. He also wanted the game off against Swindon on the night of the 9/11 atrocities. He thought there were bigger things to worry about than striving to get through a round in the League Cup and wasn't pleased that the tie went to extra-time before we won 2-0.

He commuted from Sheffield throughout his time here because his son was settled in school. He used to leave home at 5am. I got in early enough, so did the groundsman, but the gaffer was a very early starter. He was unlikely to last too long once he had turned our fortunes round because either he was going to be head-hunted or things would go off between him and the board and he would be sacked. I knowingly asked him whether he had enjoyed his lunch out after we got wind, during 2000-01, of the fact he had met Doug Ellis after the resignation of John Gregory. I added: "No need to answer that – just take Alison with you when you get your Premier League job!" There was a lot of in-house fighting and penny-pinching at the club. I was even asked by John Wile to do a stock take – the first time in 30 odd years that had been requested of me. He and Megson didn't speak for ages and I remember Gary asking for some aspirin when he went for a meeting with the chairman. He said it was like going to the dentist. Gary had it in his mind that Paul Thompson didn't think we were ready to go up the season we actually did and was at pains to tell him you couldn't pick and choose your time. If the opportunity was there, you had to go for it. We even had a good run to the quarter-final of the FA Cup that season and had a chuckle before the third-round victory at Sunderland when the coach driver

Graham and me each found ourselves in rooms with Jacuzzis at the Marriott Hotel Durham Royal Court. We were convinced we were in the rooms Paul Thompson and John Wile should have had. Gary would have enjoyed that if relations weren't great at the time and he saw the funny side when the two top men on the board found themselves having to leave their cars further away from the entrance to the Stadium of Light than usual. His car – driven by me as far as Derby – and that of his assistant Frank Burrows were in the prime visitors' spaces.

There was a desperately poignant event away from the pitch in the middle of our first promotion-winning season – the sad, sad day on which Jeff Astle passed away. I sat and cried at home when I heard the news and didn't relish seeing Tony Brown and Bobby Hope at that afternoon's game against Walsall. I knew I'd be in tears again. That era in the 1960s was very special to me and I have such happy memories of Jeff. He was a bit of a Brylcreem Boy and lived just off West Bromwich High Street after coming from Notts County in 1964. He was always so generous and down to earth, the absolute life and soul of the dressing room. I've had some brilliant work colleagues at Albion but big Jeff and his family were more than that. So were Bomber, Hopey and Ally Robertson. I would class them as good friends.

Jason Roberts scored the only goal in the TV game against Walsall and paid a nice tribute to Jeff by wearing a special t-shirt under his blue and white stripes. That was nothing to do with me. I didn't know anything about it until after he scored and showed it off. I don't suppose any of us would have been any the wiser had he not netted the winner. Laraine and two of their three daughters came to the ground a few days later to see all the flowers and we shared a hug, a few tears and all those stories about goals, Albion fans and Reska the greyhound. Jeff could apparently have gone to Wolves, Chelsea or Manchester United but said Albion were better then than United. When his funeral took place on a rainy January afternoon, the lovely village of Netherseal near Burton-on-Trent had seen nothing like it. I felt proud and honoured to be part of the private family committal at the crematorium afterwards. It was all very touching. At the main service, I sat next to Colin Suggett, Barry Fry and the club chaplain Ken Hipkiss and filled up when the coffin was carried out. What did it was all the clapping and singing we could hear from the supporters who were outside getting soaked and following events by loudspeaker.

Our games in the 2001-02 season weren't the goal feasts Jeff had been used to playing in but it was then that we really learned how to hang on to a lead. We had 17 wins by 1-0 and Gary was keen to use whatever psychological ploys he could to squeeze something extra from the players. He put some less than complimentary comments from Martin Grainger on the notice board before we beat Birmingham (1-0, of course) and was building a good spirit, even if it was adding to my workload. I had to find clean training kit before Bob Taylor could get back on the coach after the players had literally dragged him through the mud on the morning of the victory at Burnley, then Warren Cummings found himself in the fountain at the hotel as pay-back for his part in the escapade. It was Bob's birthday and we celebrated with our best performance of the season and another victory, this time by 2-1. Gary has a big thing about keeping people's feet on the ground, so he told me not to take back any copies of the lovely photo the Burnley programme had of our chief scout Bobby Hope and Big Jeff holding the FA Cup in 1968. Of course I took several and stuck one on Gary's notice board and one on his peg for when he returned after a day off.

We would never have made it to the Premier League without Gary Megson. He was clever and could afford to be bold in his behaviour because we were winning. He was always trying to get a reaction. He sent a memo round various department heads in mid-February saying he had the oldest staff car (with more than 70,000 miles on the clock), a mobile phone that wasn't working, an office next to the gents' in the old stand while his secretary was 400 yards away in the new East Stand and nowhere to even make a cup of tea. That wasn't the only turbulence. The physio Nick Worth put his notice in after being told he needed a written requisition if a player was to have a scan. So was a director going to come in on a Saturday night or Sunday morning to sign one if a player was injured? In Don Howe's day, we could see to x-rays at the ground and a retired radiographer would come in to do them when necessary – another sign of how far ahead we were then.

With a couple of months of 2001-02 left, we were miles behind Manchester City and Wolves but looking good for the play-offs. We beat Cheltenham in the fifth round of the Cup and followed up a midweek defeat at Millwall by thrashing Portsmouth 5-0. And Gary and Frank had worried about the players looking flat before that game! We had developed a worrying knack of missing penalties but had a tremendous inspiration in Derek McInnes. He consistently lifted those around him but used to be outstanding in final preparations on a Friday. That's because we had a green shirt for the worst player in training that day and he associated the colour with Celtic. He was a huge Rangers fan. We even got a hooped shirt in as a joke – and a threat to him. Every dressing room has garments of shame like this. Ours was never washed and reeked to high heaven. Another time, we had a yellow one with the word 'Donkey' and an appropriate picture on. Derek found an ally when Ally McCoist, who was a hero at Rangers, of course, came to interview him and me for a feature for Saturday lunchtime TV.

There were only six weekends left in the season when we went to Sheffield United in mid-March. Gary seemed uptight before the game. Being a Sheffield boy obviously gave the fixture an extra edge to him and his dislike of Neil Warnock was another factor. One year, before we beat the Blades, the boss told the players to ram it down Warnock's throat by making sure they celebrated any goals in front of the visitors' dug-out. They did and Warnock was letting rip at various players in the passage at half-time. Another time, after we had narrowly won at Bramall Lane, Gary pulled the coach in at a pub or hotel just outside the city and bought a round of drinks for the whole squad. The lads would have preferred to get straight home but loosened up when he bought a second lot. He handed £600 over at the bar. That's how pleased he was to get one over his rival. There was clearly big history between the two.

Something had gone on in the past as well between Andy Johnson and our former midfielder Georges Santos, who was now a Sheffield United player. As we know, all hell let loose in the Battle of Bramall Lane and the referee Eddie Wolstenholme must have wished he hadn't rushed back from a break in Tenerife to officiate it. Georges just flipped after going on as a substitute and immediately caught AJ with an awful high challenge. He was sent off and showed a side of his personality we had never seen. He was a gentle giant at The Hawthorns but found this frightening inner strength and it took God knows how many people to bring him down that afternoon. I ushered Andy, who had to come off and didn't play for several weeks, into the dressing room, shut the outer door and locked the inside one. He was scared Georges might go in and pick up some crutches as weapons. All told, United had three players ordered off and two more walked off injured. The match was abandoned a few minutes before the end and there was a horrible feeling for a while that we might have to replay it. Gary came in afterwards to tell all the players they were barred from speaking to the press and would be fined two weeks' wages if they did. He was furious about some of the things being shouted from the Sheffield bench and went to the trouble of getting a lip-reader in to see if he could prove exactly what instructions were forthcoming. Andy Johnson was just thankful to get home in something like one piece after being the victim of that tackle and then having big Georges hunting for him. Their paths did cross again. At Ipswich a year or two later, I told Andy I was talking to Georges in the corridor and being nice to him. He didn't want to encounter him and said 'You bastard!' when he realised I had been winding him up. The match passed off quietly.

The gap between us and Wolves in the race for second place was closing and, in the space of 24 hours or so, we made huge inroads into their lead. The Football League officially awarded us the three points from Bramall Lane, then Bob Taylor headed the winner late at Nottingham Forest and had us starting to believe we could go up automatically. Gary gave the players a right roasting at half-time at Forest and said later he should have had an Oscar for his performance. I can't remember what he said but it worked. He was brilliant at extracting every psychological edge going. If anyone from Wolves said something out of place – and that seemed to be quite often – he would have it cut out and pinned on the dressing room wall. When we heard they were planning a trip to the Bahamas to celebrate winning promotion, that just added to the determination to overtake them.

There was an incredible shift in momentum. The more they stumbled from what looked an uncatchable position, the stronger we became. We finished with seven wins and a draw from eight games – and it would have been eight victories had Jordao's shot against Rotherham not been ridiculously ruled as not having crossed the line, when it was a yard over. Easter Monday was a big day. Wolves kicked off early at home to Manchester City and Gary asked me to let him know the score as soon as I found it out but to say nothing to the players if Wolves had won. I returned to the dressing room beaming and with my thumbs up, so he knew we were in business. We were at Coventry and won with another goal from Bob, this time an early one. We were level on points with three matches to go but all the momentum was with us. Gary and I had a superstition thing going for a while. I spotted two magpies near the Tom Silk

Building once before a game we won well, so he decided he had to do the same before subsequent matches. He even stopped his car once near Forge Lane on the way in and was quite frustrated when he couldn't see any, so I printed two off the Internet and stuck them on the board to satisfy him.

Any bit of help that was going, we seized on it.

Chapter Eighteen

A Pre-Match Like No Other

Our Sunday draw against Rotherham took us one point clear of Wolves after they had lost on the Friday, then we played first the following weekend when we went to Bradford. Some thought the omens weren't good when we were denied access to the pitch we planned to use next to the Marriott Hotel because some gypsies were on it. My insistence that it was a good-luck sign didn't look so ridiculous when SuperBob won that stoppage-time penalty which Igor Balis tucked away. It's just as well Scott Dobie didn't have to take it. He was in a cold sweat; so nervous it's untrue. I've never seen anyone in such a state. We had been missing penalties left, right and centre and he hoped it hadn't got round to him again. I often miss goals at the end of halves because of my duties and was in the dressing room when Igor memorably did his stuff. There was a high window overlooking the pitch, so I opened it to see our fans boing-boinging. It was a great sight and the victory left us just needing to win our final game, at home to Crystal Palace, to be sure of going up.

No-one was more nervous in our build-up than Adrian Chiles. There was a noticeable disbelieving pause in the conversation when Sheffield Wednesday's manager Terry Yorath kidded him along in a BBC radio interview by saying he had a catalogue of injuries and was going to have to field a severely weakened team on the last day at home to Wolves. Adrian fell for it good and proper. His stomach was obviously doing somersaults. A couple of weeks earlier, he had been interviewing Millwall's manager Mark McGhee before their home game against Wolves and promised him a delivery of quality wine if his team got a result; a full case if they won and half of one if they drew. Steve Claridge scored the only goal of the game and Adrian said it was the best £950 he had ever spent.

In the countdown to the Palace game, someone saw some comments in the paper from Clinton Morrison, supposedly saying he would like to do Wolves a favour by beating us as he was friends with Mark Kennedy from the Republic of Ireland squad. Mmmm.....time to find a bit more room on the notice board. And Dave Jones had been quoted somewhere as saying: "West Brom have had their day. We will have ours." That was on display as well. Underneath, in a coloured pen, Gary wrote: "Not fuckin' today, they won't!" He was at his best in the dressing room before this game and got it pumped up like never before. There was a right din, with the lads hollering, clapping their hands and urging each other on. They couldn't wait to go out there and get the job finished but Gary wasn't quite done. In the most famous pre-match pep talk in my 51 years, he asked: "Who do you play for? Do you play for West Brom? Do you play for your team-mates? Do you play for Gary Megson? Do you play for Frank Burrows, or the rest of the staff?" Then he said: "This is who you play for." And, on cue, I pulled the dressing room door open to let in all the wives and kids. As much as our fans were willing the lads over the line, he reckoned a reminder of family love and responsibilities was the best way to guarantee a strong performance.

Only a few of us, including Frank, were in on it. Our daughter Alison, who was Gary's secretary, had been asked to ring all the partners to tell them of the plan and to urge them to say nothing to their other halves. It had to be a secret and it worked a treat. Russell Hoult's baby wasn't the only one in tears. Gary reckoned even Bob Taylor was welling up. I was given permission to record it all and have had to do a careful editing job to make it relatively suitable for family reading here. "Everyone in, come on. Come on, kids," he says, ushering the nervous visitors into some space in the dressing room. "Right, I'll try to do this without swearing." Turning to the players and gesturing at the ladies and children, he says: "This is who you play for. West Brom, yes. The manager, yes. Team-mates, yes. But these people are who you play for most of all. They want you to win more than anybody else on this earth. But they don't want you to win for them. They want you to win for you. They know it's what you want. All football people are selfish. They move round the country and take kids out of school where they are probably very happy. Our lifestyle has to come first.....they are the rules. But today is your chance to give it back and make it worthwhile for these people. You win this match for them."

As the families were leaving the room, the hollering started again and one or two kids began crying. Above all the commotion, Gary is bellowing: "You play for your wife! You play for your children! THIS is what it's all about!" On the tape, I can hear loads of shouting, clapping and the clatter of studs on the floor. He also names a few names...... "Larus Sigurdsson, Premiership player. Bob Taylor, Premiership player. Neil Clement, Premiership player." It's stirring stuff.

The gaffer was kind enough to give Alison a nice mention in his press conference afterwards. She had ushered all the family members from the lounge where they congregated, and kept them in the corridor outside the dressing room until I was given the nod to open the door. She had also organised 16 Baggie Birds and a few other cuddly toys for the little ones, and there was one humorous aside. When the dressing room was relatively quiet, one of the youngsters tugged on his mum's leg and said: "He's written a rude word on the board." The one thing that had been overlooked in the whole military-style operation was removing the message Gary had printed in rather industrial language in response to the Dave Jones article.

With the visitors gone, the frequent use of the f word restarted – from the players as well. "We don't want to lose a fuckin' tackle. We don't want to lose a header. We don't want to lose a second ball. They get nothing from us today. Nothing. Come on boys!" There was also a mention of the fact the season had been going for more than 250 days and they mustn't blow it now. "You have come from nowhere and we have come to this, just this," Gary added. "Today is special. It's special. You become special if you win this game. You leave this dressing room as First Division players and you return as Premiership players. You have been playing against Gillingham, Stockport and Grimsby. When you come back, you could be looking forward to facing Manchester United and Arsenal. Don't fuckin' waste it now!" And there was a reminder to look at that notice board to see how they had been written off.

It was a strong squad and we were confident we would win. We had Big Dave, Handsworth-born and bred, breathing fire and uttering a few pleasantries to Clinton Morrison in the tunnel on the way out. Without giving all our secrets away, I could suggest that Danny Dichio might have joined in the welcome, which went something like: "Would you rather go to the World Cup this summer, Clinton, or to the hospital?" The lads were saying afterwards that he had barely had a kick. Wolves needed to win at Sheffield Wednesday at the same time to put us under real pressure and Gary left no stone unturned. His son Simon had a mate who was a big Wednesday fan and he gave him a tenner to keep him up to date with events at Hillsborough. When my assistant 'Bamber' Gascoigne appeared with the news that Wolves had scored inside 47 seconds, before we had even kicked off, Gary said: "Tell that James to stop messing about." Alarmingly, it was true but we rose above the tension and apprehension by leading with a goal from Big Dave after a quarter of an hour or so.

I had my tape running again at half-time. Gary was calmer. He said (some expletives deleted): "Don't let the tempo drop. That pitch is huge because of what you have done. At the moment, it's a case of 'we have an attack, they have an attack.' They have some decent players (he names Akinbiyi and Popovic) but the next goal gets you in the fuckin' Premiership. They will go. One more goal and they will go. We're nearly there. We're nearly there. All Trevor Francis (Palace's manager) gets is this talk now and they will remember it for ten minutes, tops. Then they will forget it. We are 1-0 up and we have one foot in there. Don't do anything different. Keep your shape and go direct, like I said. If we lose our shape, we've got ten men. At free-kicks, concentrate! A lot of goals come from them. Neil Clement....you're getting good at them. Concentrate. Make them count. Get another clean sheet. We have done it at Coventry, we have done it at Bradford. We have done it 20 odd times because we're good at it. While it stays like this at 1-0, you never know, so get the next goal. The next goal makes you Premiership players. You come in 45 minutes from now as Premiership players."

True to Gary's words, set-pieces did it for us. A free-kick had led to the first goal and SuperBob tucked in the second after Clem's shot from another had been saved. What a day it was! Fantastic! The best. Wolves drew 2-2 but that didn't matter a jot. Eddie Wolstenholme was again the ref and went from having only 17 people on the pitch in the Battle of Bramall Lane to having about 15,000 on the turf here. There was a massive invasion by our fans at the end and he saw it coming. He made sure he was near the tunnel when he blew the whistle, so he could get to the dressing rooms intact. Amazing! We had turned an 11-point deficit on Wolves into a final three-point lead in the space of 43 unbelievable days and were in the Premier League for the first time. The only disappointment was the lack of a proper representation from the directors afterwards to say well done. Gary complained there wasn't even a phone call, certainly no sign of any champagne from the club. I had to go up to the restaurant to get some beer because the champers handed out in the dressing room either by Sky or the Football League was used just by the players in the usual way for spraying each other while the cameras rolled or clicked away.

We were back in on the Tuesday and things were flat. It was manic enough with the players rushing around getting shirts signed by each other as souvenirs but I had to tell Jeremy Peace, who wasn't chairman then, and Joe Brandrick how disappointed the lads had been that no-one had come over from the East Stand to join in the congratulations on match day. The mood was so unexpectedly down that a member of staff put a sign up in her office saying: "Don't forget: We have been promoted, not relegated." John Wile asked for the players to go out for a team photograph and they refused. Eventually, Gary persuaded them it would do more harm than good if they didn't comply but I don't think there were many smiles on it. At least not genuine ones. It's as if all the euphoria lasted only a few hours rather than the few days it should have done. Gary's stock was very high and he was in demand. He was named as the League Managers Association Championship Manager of the Year but, when he went to one dinner, he chose to sit on a separate table to our directors. That summed up the differences behind the scenes.

We certainly hadn't bought our way to promotion and I remember Gary saying he was delighted for me going to the Premier League. He was also proud to have done it for true Albion legends like Bobby Hope – our chief scout for many years – and Tony Brown; even in the company of Jill from the offices and Laraine Astle, you could see how much it meant to him. And there were some celebrations. A few days later, we had a cold but thankfully dry open top bus tour from the ground to Oldbury Town Hall and I had to get Gary two giant hands to wave from the balcony. The vehicle was awful…..the Ribena Road Show Coach, we called it. It was multi-coloured and there was a TV advert on at the time that gave rise to the Ribena name.

The players organised a trip to Spain for themselves and my plans for a holiday were based around getting the address of some apartments in Portugal off Jordao. We had a 10 per cent rise for winning promotion but there was turmoil behind the scenes. Even before the row over the players' bonuses for the Premier League, we had the changeover of chairman and all the manoeuvring that brought, with members of the board taking sides with Paul Thompson or the rising power, Jeremy Peace. Brendon Batson came back as managing director and Mike O'Leary arrived as chief executive. I wrote in my diary on June 27 that things were the worst I'd known in 42 years. I even thought we'd be using the promotion-winning kit in the Premier League. I had a meeting with the HR (human resources) man Neil Smart and was given a contract of employment for the first time. I never signed it.

When my mum passed away on July 4, Gary told me to take some time off and said he'd fine me if I turned up at work. He could see things had been building up. We had no training kit and no match kit and Carol had been bad in bed. On top of that, my assistant Andy Tiernan was about to leave. I wasn't happy at having to order the kit as that job had been taken off me and should now have been the responsibility of the marketing department. It was far from the ideal build-up to a season back in the top flight but the lure of the Premier League was soon brought home to me. I was loading the skips on to the coach after the opening-day game at Manchester United when I heard the fans chanting 'David, David' and asking for various things to be signed. I thought: 'Wow, this is a bit different....a kit-man being hunted for his autograph.' Then I noticed Mr Beckham, with Brooklyn, standing beside me in the tunnel. I was nevertheless a bit caught up in it all. I got Sir Alex Ferguson to sign my programme and Leeds manager Terry Venables did the same, along with our players, on our first home programme the weekend after.

Chapter Nineteen

Premier League Crash Landing

What worked brilliantly in the Championship over two seasons proved to be inadequate now we were with the elite for the first time in more than a quarter of a century. It took Manchester United three-quarters of the game to break us down on the opening day but we were then well beaten by Leeds and even more heavily at Arsenal. Although we followed up with three victories in a row (all 1-0!), it was the last day of November before we won again. Gary Megson tried what he could and had a pop before the game at Newcastle in early October about players costing others their bonuses with their performances. We lost up there and Bob Taylor and Danny Dichio, who didn't play in that game, were changing with the second team on the Monday. He could fall out with people quickly and, as early as July 1, had some cause for complaint when Jordao and Brian Jensen reported back after their summer break and failed the beep test that measures the players' capacity to do a series of short bursts inside a certain time.

I was with Andy Johnson at a meeting of the Kidderminster branch of the Supporters Club not long ago when he took Gary off to a tee from the day he came in at half-time, turned to his trusty assistant and said: "Frank, the lunatics have taken over the asylum. They're running it good and proper, yet I don't hear my phone ringing with bids for any of them." It was the gaffer's way of letting them know he was distinctly displeased. There was an element of bullying about what Gary did but Frank had said after we went up: "We can't bully them now. They're Premier League." You could always rely on AJ to lighten the mood. He once super-glued Geoff Horsfield's boots to the floor. He was amazed Gary had brought him to West Brom at all because their parting at Norwich was less than amicable. Apparently they said farewell with a

141

flaming row across the manager's desk. Gary would like the way he stood up to him, though. He didn't like wishy-washy characters.

The players reckon he would have them in on a day off to practise if they messed up their set-pieces. He'd go through them a hundred times on the training ground, then say: "Right, thanks for dragging me in on my day of rest, now f*&@ off!" There were lighter moments, like when Simon Miotto went in the plunge bath as he was keeping it topped up with ice for the players on the day of England's victory in the Rugby World Cup final in Australia. I and Bamber kept well out of the way. The squad were also fitted with special tights, even for sleeping in, so I told them not to forget to take them off before they went to the loo. Life was always interesting with Gary and I was pleased to meet his dad Don once or twice in the office. He did some scouting for him and played for Sheffield Wednesday on the day of one of my first Albion matches. He was calmer than Gary. Then again, he's older and has had more time to mellow.

After we were relegated and were going strongly for promotion again, Gary said he was going to toughen the squad up by taking them on a four-day trip to Exeter. He wouldn't have been impressed with our reserve keeper Joe Murphy moaning about having to do four laps of the pitch as a training exercise after being unused as a substitute in an FA Cup defeat at Nottingham Forest tie. I worked out that that was about £500 a lap considering he was probably on about £2,000 bonus for being on the bench. We had suffered a dip in form and Gary had it in mind he needed some wins, otherwise he was out. The mood was a bit grim and we heard while we were in Devon that Gary Shelton, who stayed behind at the club, had apparently sent the players home because there was no-one to put the kit out for the young lads. The Sunday Mercury picked the story up. Things were lightened when Frank Burrows went for a run over the moors and spotted a holdall, which he picked up and handed in. He hadn't realised that 40 members of the military were engaged in an exercise, with the holdall as their target.

Rob Hulse left his boots behind after Exeter, so we packed them and hid them until the Friday to teach him a lesson and encourage him to look after them. He was handed them back for the game at Burnley and was promptly sent off. My diary shows we were in a spell where strange things happened to players. Joe Murphy was charged £90 by a locksmith who was only there ten minutes and Jason Koumas's little one flushed a bunch of house and car keys down the toilet. All this a few weeks after we had took two of our groundsmen on the coach for the draw at Crystal Palace.

When we went up the second time, Gary made sure there was some champagne on hand to celebrate properly. And, because our Premier League return was secured on a Saturday lunchtime when Sunderland failed to win at Wigan, the lads were treated to a glass of bubbly before they went out and won 2-0 at home to Bryan Robson's Bradford side. Lee Hughes scored that day but had a huge cloud hanging over him after his serious motoring offence. Other engagements during the legal process meant he was chauffeured up to the game at Preston in early February by my assistant Bamber – then he was sacked by the club after being sentenced to six years in the very month we returned to the Premier League. In my possession is a letter written a few days after we had opened with a draw at Blackburn, stating: Number LG9884 Name Hughes, Wing D. From HM Prison, Ashwell, Oakham, Rutland. "To the boys: How's it going, boys, all the best for the season – wished I was there. Just watching Coronation Street in my cell with my cell mate Dave – he is a friend of my mates. Played five-a-side football against the screws on Saturday when you played against Blackburn. Not a bad result (well done). Been to the gym here everyday because nothing else to do. Just to get out of my cell. It's been ok here I have had no trouble. Just people shouting from different wings about me. Everybody has looked after me. If anyone wants to write, my prison number is at the top. Any mags welcomed (and stamps)."

Back at the club, Jason Koumas drove the gaffer to distraction. He was late reporting for the pre-season trip to Denmark and then forgot his runners on two successive days after we had returned home. He was a good player but high maintenance. He didn't drive and was often relying on his brother to get him to places on time. He didn't figure much back in the top flight and we struggled again. I was at Merry Hill shopping with Carol on October 26 when Gary phoned to say he had been sacked. I said I was sorry, if he was. He knew it was coming. He had given the players a right bollocking during the 3-0 defeat at Crystal Palace a few days earlier and Frank had told them on the Monday to put down their cards – a reference to the fact they had played all the way back at the weekend. The defenders were made to watch a video of the game on the Monday and the forwards on the Tuesday.

After Gary was dismissed, he asked me to empty his office at the training ground before anyone else got to it. It seemed strange being there and seeing no car in the space marked 'manager'. I located a photo of him with the first promotion-winning team and put it in safe keeping. I also retrieved some of his training kit as well as a Lucozade bottle which I marked 'brandy only'. I was amazed to receive a phone call from Joe Brandrick asking me to keep all his kit as some would go in the East Stand museum and some would be sold on the club website. In one breath, Joe was saying it was a sad time and in another he was thinking of making money from his departure. The following day, we transferred Gary's folders and other belongings to Frank's boot. It was a fittingly crazy way to end a controversial but highly eventful and successful era. And it obviously wasn't only at The Hawthorns that his work had been noted. His old mobile was by now being used by the reception staff and Wolves rang it three times asking to speak to him on the day they sacked Dave Jones.

Chapter Twenty

Stunned By A Sickening Blow

Bryan Robson was certainly well connected in the game. His magnificent playing career had seen to that. When Mick McCarthy left the Republic of Ireland job after his bust-up with Roy Keane, Bryan spoke to Roy, Andy Townsend and Denis Irwin for a briefing before going to an interview for the national job. He didn't get it but had Ron Atkinson in his corner when we were manager-seeking again in the autumn of 2004 in the wake of Gary Megson's departure. Gordon Strachan, Glenn Hoddle and Gerard Houllier were also linked at a time when Wolves were in the market for a new boss as well. Hoddle and possibly Bryan, who were former England midfield colleagues, were in the running for both posts. Bryan got the nod here and as his no 2 brought in Nigel Pearson, who had been his captain for part of the time at Middlesbrough. We lost at home to Boro in their first match in charge when Kanu somehow missed from a yard or two right at the end with an equaliser and a respectable draw beckoning.

Monday, November 15 is underlined in red in my diary. It's a day I will never forget. Our daughter Alison, an Albion fan all her life and the manager's secretary at the club for more than ten years going back to Keith Burkinshaw's time in charge, was called into the office of our head of human resources Neil Smart and handed an envelope informing her she was out of work. Things were apparently being done differently in future and her position was no longer there. They informed her what she was entitled to and told her to report back at 10am the following day with a colleague of her choice. Instead, she took her sister Clare. I literally never slept a wink that night and felt so lousy next morning with a headache and with my stomach in a knot that I finished at lunchtime and went to the doctor's to get my blood pressure checked. The secretary Dr John Evans could hardly look at me when he came to the training ground. Alison phoned Gary Megson, informed him of the news and made it clear she didn't blame him in any way. He urged me to make sure I wasn't next. He told the physio Nick Worth, who had been persuaded to withdraw his earlier notice, and myself to keep our noses clean, get in a union and seek some legal help.

Alison, who had previously done some match-day catering work at the club and then taken a full-time job in the ticket office despite having trained as a medical secretary, had seen to the paperwork when we signed Warren Cummings from Chelsea on deadline day in March, 2001, as the directors and Gary were in Sheffield. She also typed up all the contracts when Phil Gilchrist signed on loan with a few minutes to spare after she had sat around waiting nearly all day, only for everything to happen at the end. We were now told, though, that lap-tops meant managers could be more self-sufficient and less reliant on a secretary. But when I went to see Bryan to tell him I would continue to do my job to the best of my ability, I soon learned he could only perform the basic tasks on his computer. He was soon asking who was going to do his letters, open his post and make arrangements for games. He wasn't happy at all – and had only been there a few days. We had known each other for more than 30 years and I suppose I had been a senior figure during his teenage years, so there was a strong bond between us.

I had no interest in work while all this was going on and sat in a haze through the game at Arsenal, where Jeremy Peace came to the hotel on the night before for a meal. Fortunately, I had already eaten with the players by then and didn't see him. I'm not sure the club deserved her support but Alison came to watch the 3-0 defeat against Manchester United the following weekend. Darren Moore showed his concern but, when Portsmouth scored a last-minute winner against us, I could at least console myself with the feeling that they had stuck it up whoever had taken the decision that our eldest daughter was no longer required at the club she grew up loving. When Charlton won at The Hawthorns on December 11, I saw only two minutes of the game and that included them scoring the only goal. I just wasn't interested. Danny Murphy was refused admission to the players' lounge afterwards and chuntered: "This is a First Division club heading back to the First Division." In my downbeat state of mind, I found it hard to disagree. So many people sympathised with

Alison and the Supporters Club presented her with two engraved brandy glasses as a thank-you for all she had done for them. But she was even told on Christmas Eve that she couldn't go into the offices at The Hawthorns to hand out cards and presents.

Maybe the worry of that situation helped explain why I had a big bust-up with Geoff Horsfield after the game at Birmingham in the December. The club had paid £7,000 for 27 of us to stay overnight in Sutton beforehand, then we played badly and lost 4-0. When Geoff was asking for his shirt afterwards, we had more than a few words that culminated in him saying: "Shut up and do your job." I retorted: "If you'd start doing yours, we wouldn't be bottom of the League." Some players, including Artim Sakiri, didn't think there should be a Christmas party after that performance. I agreed with him but they still went off for their night out. Actually it was a day and night because they left training on the Monday in their fancy dress, next stop the King Arthur pub. Bryan gave them too much trust and I feared it would rebound on him. Bernt Haas's departure from the do made headlines in The Sun. He was resplendent in his Robin Hood outfit and blond wig and apparently the worse for wear. So much so that the taxi driver rang the paramedics just to make sure he was okay. It wasn't the only time a fancy-dress occasion led to a spot of bother. Steve Watson turned up in either his Batman or Superman suit when we were flying to Dubai for a mid-season break. Bryan wasn't amused. He thought it was taking the idea of a bonding trip too far. Kanu had taken some liberties of his own when he failed to turn up for the game against Manchester United not long after the gaffer's arrival and also gave training a miss on the Sunday and Monday. The players sat in judgement on such matters and fined him a week's wages.

When Bryan got busy in the market, he did so to good effect. He liked Kevin Campbell for his personality and dressing-room influence and also went for some younger blood by using his Manchester United connections in taking Kieran Richardson on loan as well as paying Burnley good money for Richard Chaplow. We had loads of experience up front with Kanu, Geoff Horsfield and Robbie Earnshaw already there. We picked up in the Great Escape year after a bonding trip to Orlando. Earnie scored a hat-trick as a substitute when the club rewarded the fans further with a free day out to Charlton organised by our sponsors T-Mobile. The famous theme music became part of our match-day routine and it seemed amazing we were still bottom with a game to go, given the way we celebrated after Robbie's penalty earned us a 1-1 draw at Old Trafford in the penultimate fixture. Clearly it was a time for substitutions of impact. Tomasz Kusczak played a blinder when going on for the injured Russell Hoult against United but didn't have much to do when we beat Portsmouth 2-0 the weekend after to stay up on an afternoon of unbelievable tension. Horse had said to Bryan at half-time: "I always score important goals." He was sent on as sub and did it again almost straightaway. We were relying on the fans behind the dug-out for information from Crystal Palace's game at Charlton and went through agonies as they took the lead and then conceded the equaliser. We stood around for several minutes at the end of our game before learning that it had finished 2-2 at The Valley and we were safe. There wasn't any shortage of champagne that day. Bryan got a right soaking and the mood of celebration continued when Ronnie Wallwork was presented with the Player of the Year award.

I put money on us to pull off the Great Escape because, when Portsmouth's kit-man had texted us about what colours they would be wearing, he said it was a nothing match for them. That convinced me we should be okay. I remember backing us to win and having another flutter on us stopping up. It was allowed then and I had a bit of fun some time afterwards with one of Bryan Robson's subsequent signings, John Hartson. I didn't realise how much he was in debt – it was hundreds of thousands of pounds. Innocently thinking he just enjoyed the occasional flutter, I used to get tips from Peter Chapple-Hyam, the Albion-supporting trainer from Dudley, and share them with John. My big day came when Peter won The Derby with Authorise. I backed it at 16/1 after his jockey Frankie Dettori had told Peter he would win. It was the most I've ever won in a bet and Peter often used to tell us if he had a horse in particularly good shape. Another of his stable won once at 8/1 and Big John gave me a nice thank-you after backing it. Going a long way back, Peter came to the hotel when we were playing at Oxford in Ron Atkinson's time and loved coming on the coach with us. He was also in the Royal Box on one of the Wembley trips.

I always enjoyed chatting to Peter, having picked up my modest interest in gambling from my dad. He enjoyed the dogs and I went with him to Perry Barr. He always taught me never to chase my losses and to only gamble what I could afford to lose. Most Saturdays, I go to the bookies, where I have an account, and have a bet on the horses. Of the vices – drink, gambling and sex – I always went for a bet on account that it tended to last the longest. I don't smoke.

You'll notice me talking more about my wins than my losses but I'll be honest and admit I've probably lost more than I've won. I've had the buzz from it for many years, though, as well as a good run for my money. I do the coupon now, go to Cheltenham most years and sometimes to York. John Hartson got me fixed up with some corporate hospitality one year. The lads generally enjoy a bet – and a few of them own horses or at least part of one. One prominent player from the last decade or so flew with a jockey to a meeting in Dubai on a day off.

Before the authorities made it illegal for football people to bet on matches and competitions they were involved in, I was never afraid to use a bit of inside knowledge to my advantage. Once I came back from putting the kit out at Villa in Big Ron's second spell here and saw some betting slips which had George Reilly at 33/1 to score the first goal. The bookies thought he was going to carry on playing at centre-half, so Ron, knowing he was switching him up front on a hunch, gave me £20 and I went and put it on at William Hill's in Smethwick High Street. The ball came across at 0-0 – I think that's how it finished – and George stretched but couldn't quite turn it in. It would have been £660. I didn't miss out when I saw Ossie Ardiles arrive at the club in 1992 either. I hadn't been told he was getting the job but, when I noticed him there, I thought he was worth a punt at 3/1, especially as the board were looking for a purer style following Bobby Gould's departure. I even talked my bookie into giving me another point on the odds and staked £20, which came back to me several times over. And when Ron was about to be installed at Villa, I was cutting his lawns, so I wasn't going to pass up that opportunity to make a few bob.

Frank Burrows once made a point of saying he fancied Lee Hughes to score the first goal against Sheffield Wednesday. The boss had had a go at him around that time for smiling when we were losing and I was tipped off about how much that had fired him up. Another win, this time £90 at 7/2.....thank-you very much. I knew times when we were flying and I backed us to do the treble in 1978-79. We expected to win every match. Equally, though, I'm a realist and have backed against Albion if I knew we were in bad shape. I recall putting money on Wolves to win at The Hawthorns in 1983-84 and they did. They were double-figure odds because Wolves hadn't won all season and it was getting towards Christmas. I also backed Liverpool at 40/1 with Coral's to win 5-0 at our place one Boxing Day as well as winning both halves. They did and I filled my pockets. Of course I wanted us to win but a trip to the bookies was an opportunity to make a bit of money. I went with my feeling about the team. Once we were playing in the cup in midweek and the League on a Saturday and I knew we were putting a weakened side out in a tie we would normally be expected to win. We lost 2-0. There was a little compensation for me. Without knowing it, Paul McShane might easily have delivered big time for me in an FA Cup tie at home to Leeds in 2006-07. I bet on him to score our last goal in a 3-1 win at odds of 175/1. I got the result right but he went and got the bloody first goal instead! Another time, I backed us to win 3-1 and Jason Koumas to score the first goal. Both legs of the bet came up and I won at 66/1.

Betting on us to stay up again in 2005-06 would have been unrewarding. After the Great Escape, our struggles continued, this time with a less happy outcome. We went down and Bryan Robson was sacked a few weeks into the following season. Another exciting roller-coaster ride was about to begin.......

Chapter Twenty One

Mowbray: A Good Fit

Considering how strong we were at home in the first few months of Tony Mowbray's reign and the fact we had won well at Ipswich and Crystal Palace when he was about to take over, it seemed crazy that we were so poor away. From the time he was appointed in the October to well into January, we were dreadful travellers. He even changed the routine by flying the players to more distant locations but there was no improvement. We lost at Southend on New Year's Day and managed only a draw at Plymouth. I have my own special memories of Roots Hall. The dressing rooms there were antiquated and there was no room for the skips, so they had to go in the gym under the stand. While I'm at it, Crewe and Bradford also used to be bad for getting the skip from the coach to the dressing room and negotiating the steep steps at Watford was a nightmare.

That day at Southend, we had a visit from the drug squad afterwards and it took so long for Jonathan Greening and John Hartson to provide the necessary samples that it was just as well we had a charter flight. The team would have missed the plane otherwise. We had time to kill and Brian Dear, now the catering manager at Southend, seemed to delight in telling us after providing us with our food for the journey home how he once scored five for West Ham against us in the mid-1960s. I had Jason Koumas as company on the bus. As well as not driving, he didn't enjoy flying. Tony and Mark Venus liked him, though, especially when he was cutting in from the left on to his right foot and preparing to shoot. Veno also had a high regard for Diomansy Kamara but they were troubled by the fact the players didn't want to do sprints on a Friday and some of those from further afield were more concerned with getting home early and beating the traffic back to Liverpool, Manchester or London. Players generally get away with too much now. One of them didn't want to play in one game because he had a graze. John Kaye would have had him round the throat for saying he wasn't fit because of that.

It was in Tony's first part season that we kept playing Wolves; five times in all, starting with his first Albion match. It was at Molineux after the second or third of them that I was able to introduce Alison to him. She was by now working at Wolves as assistant to the secretary Richard Skirrow and travelled back on their coach with Mick McCarthy's secretary Fay after they had won 4-1 at Leicester on the last afternoon of the regular League season – the same day that we thrashed Barnsley 7-0. It was Wolves v Albion in the play-offs. This might have been the season Darren Moore was locked in with our fans at the end of one game at Molineux. No wonder he asked Alison if he could have tickets among the Wolves fans next time he was going to watch us there. Much to our fans' delight, we won four out of five of the Black Country derbies in 2006-07, including both legs of the play-off semi-final.

The latter success meant we were off to the new Wembley for the first time. Actually, it was my second trip there. A few weeks earlier, I had been a guest of Umbro when the stadium reopened for football with the England v Italy under-21 international. Ray Stubbs kindly gave me a mention over the microphone in one of the corporate rooms and got me a round of applause by saying I had worked for Albion for 47 years and was still going strong. We were favourites for the final against Derby, although our League meetings that season had been tight, and I had no nerves before the game, or during it for that matter. That was despite the irritation of the club paying for 30 suits for players and immediate staff for the day and us realising there wasn't one for Bamber and me. It seemed quite ironic as we were the ones who were meant to make sure everyone else looked the part. The players called it a nonsense and said they would have a whip-round to kit us out the same. Joe Corrigan was particularly adamant we should go with it but I refused on principle and said I didn't mind sticking out like a sore thumb if the club didn't mind.

There were hassles on the pitch as well. We lost the toss for choice of kits, so Derby were allowed to wear their normal white shirts and we had to change. I took three different kits and had heard it suggested we might play in black tops and white shorts. But I suspected the officials would decide that that might have made the pitch look like a chessboard and wouldn't allow it, so I packed yellow and green as well as blue and white, just in case. I was short of one or two bits in yellow and green and got them named up and completed with a JD logo on the back of the shorts. In the end, we were in all black and Derby in their normal strip. I also spent the first part of Friday morning in the club shop putting 'boing boing' on sweaters and wet tops for extra players and staff, then it turned out we were having new warm-up and travel gear. It was all a bit of a headache. The club shop was heaving with fans treating themselves to something for the big day and, on top of all that, my mother-in-law was moving house. Finding someone free to do the printing for me was out of the question and, although Umbro would do it if asked and send it back next day by courier, they charged for the service. So I operated the machine myself. It wasn't common knowledge that I had one in my kit room for a while before it went to the warehouse when the Halfords Lane Stand was redeveloped. I thought the board would swamp me if they knew I had one, thinking they would save money. My friend Tony Lloyd, who worked in the warehouse for a time, came in and helped. The device in my room was for emergency use, such as a new signing being made when the club shop was shut.

Derby's people were at the stadium when we arrived with our kit and I was really impressed with the place. The organisation was first-class and I took some photos of the black shirts and shorts hanging up. Peter Chapple-Hyam had rung to ask for a ticket for his driver, so Neil Clement sorted that out and I spoke to the three former Albion players in Derby's team – Big Dave, Paul Peschisolido and Julian Darby. I went back to the hotel and had a chat with Frank Skinner and Adrian Chiles but the day ended in disappointment for us all with a 1-0 defeat. A couple of days later, before Carol and I went off to Corfu for a fortnight, I had a chat with Tony and he reckoned that not everyone was pulling together. There was a feeling several players would go now we knew we would again be playing in the Championship and that's exactly what happened.

Credit Tony for building a title-winning team the following season because he virtually dismantled the Wembley side, or had it dismantled for him. Only four players from the team beaten by Derby started at Burnley on the opening day in August, 2007 – Dean Kiely, Zoltan Gera, Jonathan Greening and Kevin Phillips. Paul McShane, Chris Perry, Jason Koumas, Diomansy Kamara and the on-loan Sam Sodje had all left. Paul Robinson failed a medical at Wigan and stayed to have a very good season. There was more of a cosmopolitan appearance to the squad and Filipe Teixeira looked the part from the day he made his debut in a friendly at Northampton. That was also the summer Tony brought in Chris Brunt and James Morrison, with a move for Graham Dorrans being made a few months later. It was quite a turnover of players.

The 2007-08 campaign wasn't without its quirkiness. When we set off for a pre-season friendly at Bristol Rovers, we used a hotel three junctions past the city and we 'over-shot' again when we stopped not far from the Hull City ground before we played Scunthorpe in late September. At this point, I probably made a note to buy a map of the British Isles to hand to the people whose job it was to choose and book our hotels. We had no objection, though, when Millwall asked to use the visitors' dressing room at The Hawthorns before they trained in The Dome in Halfords Lane for their game at Walsall the following day.

A meeting with another London club, Charlton, brought problems over kit when they refused to send their keeper out in a silver jersey for our FA Cup tie there and insisted on him wearing green. I thought Dean Kiely was going to have to go out in a navy t-shirt until I found an old silver top at the bottom of our skip. It had no number and was a 'blood shirt' – there just in case Dean had a cut of some kind and had to replace his. If Luke Steele had gone on as sub, he would have had to wear Dean's but I don't know what would have happened had Dean gone off with a bad gash. The referee had said before the kick-off he wasn't happy with both keepers wearing green and we could see his point. If one of them went up for a set-piece late on, there was the risk of the officials struggling to distinguish between the two. The ill-feeling with Charlton persisted. When they came to us for the replay, they turned up at the ground without asking permission to lay their kit out and I gave them the cold shoulder. 'Arrogant Londoners' is one of the headings in my diary. The tie went to penalties and, although I missed the decisive moments because I had taken sweaters out for the lads while they were standing around for the shoot-out, and then had to gather them and take them back in, I was even more pleased that night that we went through.

Considering we had such a changed squad, things ran very smoothly on the pitch. We were always up with the leaders and had no trouble scoring goals. Even when we were without nine players through injury or suspension at

Leicester in early December, Craig Beattie curled in a beauty for our late winner and the players were in high spirits when we dropped them off just down the road at the Marriott Hotel to get another bus down to London for their Christmas party. Richard Chaplow reportedly had a £4,000 bill on his credit card when they got back. Not that he had a better time than anyone else. It's just that he had stood them their bar and food outgoings on his 'flexible friend.' The strange happenings continued when we had a call from Villa asking for the loan of our fourth official's board as theirs wasn't charging. We also had a youngster called Joss Labadie who caused us a problem when we found the B wasn't working on the printing machine. On top of that, we seemed to have a surplus of Lucozade and, because we needed the storage room, I was happy to hand over some bottles to our former midfielder Gary Hackett when his Stourbridge side were playing in the FA Cup and also some to John Trewick, who was at Hereford.

The lads played some great stuff as we bombed on towards promotion and made thrilling progress in the FA Cup, winning handsomely at Coventry in the fifth round and at Bristol Rovers in the sixth. We had a bit of a wobble before going back to Wembley for the semi-final against Portsmouth and had an awkward League game at Blackpool three nights later. It was a key time and I had my work cut out. I had to pack for the Blackpool game at the same time as for Wembley because we would be travelling up there on the Monday and there would be no time to get things washed in between. Before the semi, Alison received a phone call from a contact at the FA saying there was one mascot's place going and did she know anyone who might be interested? The upshot was that Amy, the grand-daughter of our neighbour Margaret, had a day she will never forget by walking out on to the pitch with the players. Confusingly, our other neighbours Martin and Helen have a daughter Amy, who was at the game as well. I saw her and her sister Charlotte with a banner behind the goal that read: 'My Uncle Dave, WBA Kit-Man and Legend.' True to form, I took some photos of it.

There were none of the kit problems we had known before the play-off final against Derby. Both clubs wore their first-choice strips, although I've known the time when we would always have had to change on our visits to Fratton Park and the same for Portsmouth when they came here. At Wembley, we also had some fun at the expense of my assistant Bamber, who had to sit on the steps because there was no seat for him. Joe Corrigan prodded me in the chest at one point because Bamber was running to the touchline, whistling and doing all the arm signals to tell our midfielder Kim Do-Heon to prepare himself for going on as a substitute. We joked that he was doing it for the cameras. We'd known him applauding the fans before now and even joining in the huddle at the end of one game. We ribbed him that he thought he was a bloody player. Albert Morgan and his assistant Vic at Manchester United always seemed to be on TV as the cameras were pointed at Sir Alex Ferguson so much. I had joked with Derrick Jones the masseur before we went to Wembley in 2007 that I'd sit right behind Tony and asked: "Who shall I be today? Albert or Vic?" Bamber probably knows there was one time when I played up to the cameras, big time. Clare and her partner at the time, Kevin, were on holiday in Barbados and had found a bar in which to watch our live game at Fulham. I mocked up a sign on some cardboard and stood near that lovely old cottage so I was clearly visible to them when a corner was taken from that side.

We were bitterly disappointed to lose to Portsmouth by the only goal, especially as another Championship team, Cardiff, would have been waiting for us in the final. But Kanu, bless him, was true to his word in giving me his shirt after the game. I suppose it was the least he could do as he had scored a messy winner. Deflated or not, we left the dressing rooms looking like we had barely been there and swept up, just as we always did, whether it was Wembley or Wimbledon. With Tony, we cleaned up after ourselves home and away and host clubs often couldn't believe it. It was his way. He thought it was bad manners not to but we still had opponents contacting us afterwards to say thank-you. Derrick Jones the masseur would help. We started leaving a broom in the away dressing room here and some would use it, some wouldn't. You wouldn't believe the mess we sometimes found it in. It was a serious lack of respect, as if they were saying: "You should have staff to do that. It's not for us to clean up."

With the anti-climax caused by the Portsmouth result, we could have continued our stumble in the League as well because we trailed at Blackpool with nine minutes left. Then we scored three times to get us right back on track and show that we could go the distance in the promotion race. Not that I saw the key moments at Bloomfield Road. I was attending to my chores in the dressing room and missed all of our goals. When I say I've seen thousands of

Albion games down the years, what I really mean is that I've seen substantial chunks of thousands of games. I have seen relatively few kick-offs and not heard too many blows on the final whistle. It was a happy dressing room that night. The three points ensured Tony Mowbray remained content. He didn't often lose his temper. I suppose you could argue that he brought us good times and would rarely have had to give the players a piece of his mind. Most of his talks were aimed at constructive criticism and developing the feeling of togetherness. When he would vent his displeasure was if he thought someone had let the team down.

I very much liked Tony's football. He knew what the club's traditions were for playing attractively and he was a good fit. What he wasn't always so good at was making decisions. But, at QPR on the final day of our 2007-08 Championship-winning season, it was his idea that the players stripped off their all black change kit after one round of celebrations in front of our fans – and went back out to lap it all up again in our navy blue and white. He thought it was only right that the photos recording our first League title win for 88 years should show the lads in the club's famous stripes. Yet, for an FA Cup tie at Middlesbrough the previous season, he had agreed to the players' wish to play in all black when there was no reason to change from blue and white.

Tony reckoned I couldn't offend anyone and wouldn't want to. That tallies with what Johnny Giles said at my 50th anniversary dinner…..that part of the reason for me lasting so long was that we all have opinions but I knew better than most when to voice them and when to shut up. I inadvertently got Tony a fine once, though, when I rang him, not knowing he was in a team meeting and had forgotten to put his phone on silent. Not even the manager escaped that one. He was a valuable support to me and, having written a book himself, was always keen to know how mine was coming on. On a night out in Malaga, where he must have spent £400 on wining and dining various members of his staff during a mid-winter trip, he enquired as to the title and I admitted to a familiar headache. "It might just have to be 'Volume One,'" I replied. "With 'Volume Two' to follow, of course." Mark Venus enjoyed the discussion over a glass or two of wine but wasn't as happy the next morning. When he lined up in less than ideal condition with the reds in a seven-a-side match and won the ball in the air for the first time, he had a headache of the more usual kind and shouted across for the Paracetamol.

157

I was disappointed we didn't have an open-top bus tour after winning the League, as we had done in Gary Megson's time. The club might have had a double to celebrate because I sat at home watching and wondering during the Cup Final – after texting Kanu to wish him good luck. I was thinking we should have been there. We did capture some of that Wembley spirit, though. The night before Pompey beat Cardiff, there was a reunion of the 1968 team and I completed my set of players' signatures on my shirt when Chippy Clark did the honours. It was long after Alan Ashman had passed away but it was good to see his secretary Margaret Limbrick there. Alan would have been shocked by how big the current squad now was. It was huge and we had to pack 26 bags before we flew out of Birmingham for our pre-season tour in 2008. We were based in Holland, near the German border, and, for the game against Cologne at a neutral venue, there were no dedicated dressing rooms, so the players had to change 500 yards away and then walk with the fans to get to the pitch. There must have been a few autographs and photos en route because the kick-off was delayed 15 minutes. That was the trip when Roman Bednar pushed our new fitness coach Rob Harris into the pool fully clothed – not the thing I would have done when day after day of gruelling stamina work was already on the agenda.

At the start of the season, The Hawthorns was like a bomb site after extensive redevelopments had been carried out to the main stand on Halfords Lane. At the first League game or the friendly against Real Mallorca just before, people were walking round with blue hands because there was so much wet paint. It seemed to be an open thoroughfare to all and sundry and we had five shirts and a pair of shorts stolen. The Everton kit-man Jim Martin said he was going to report us to the Premier League in the August because the workmen were still doing the stairs. Bamber thought his ipod had been nicked as well but later found it in his car. My faithful assistant really copped it when he filled the team sheet in and put Luke Steele's name at no 16 instead of Luke Moore.

At this time, Dan Ashworth was the man I found myself moaning to time and time again on various matters. If it wasn't about needing heating in the new kit rooms at the ground so the strips wouldn't go damp, it was about holes in the wall, or having no plastering or paint. Dan wasn't always in the role of expert talent spotter here. He had more menial tasks as well. We had enough on our plate as we tried to catch up on facilities, good as they were becoming, and could have done without the call we had late in 2008 asking why our captain wasn't wearing a Premier League armband.

The redevelopment problems caused embarrassment for me. Behind the door where the visiting players go into the ground is a flight of stairs which prompted a succession of kit-men to ask me whether West Bromwich had been overlooked when it came to health and safety regulations. Manchester United's kit-man Albert Morgan was singing 'Premier League, you're having a laugh' at me when he was stuck on the footpath outside once with all his skips and bags while our security guy struggled with a huge bunch of keys looking for the elusive one to the shutter. I raised the matter with the secretary Darren Eales after Albert had said he was going to report us to the Premier League. He and United's goalkeeper coach Eric Steele couldn't believe it when I showed them round my kit room. They called it a cupboard. Around the same time, two worse-for-wear Middlesbrough fans got in and were asking for Gareth Southgate after we beat them 3-0 – an episode which led me to suggesting we needed more security on the dressing room doors.

With Tony Mowbray's help, I can expose as a bit of a charade all that handshaking that goes on between managers when the cameras pick them up on the touchline just before kick-off. They've nearly always met and exchanged pleasantries in the dressing room or office area well before that. Tony would invite Sir Alex Ferguson or Jose Mourinho, for example, to his office and have a long chat with him while the players were warming up. He'd be seeking to pick up one or two motivational tips while also clearing his mind for a few minutes of the stresses of the game. Then he'd go out and shake Sir Alex's hand again by the dug-outs as that public show of respect. At other times, Tony would be on his own in the dressing room half an hour or so before kick-off, listening to some Michael Buble once he had got rid of what he called the players' 'rave rubbish.'

When we went to United that season, Ronaldo came by as I was standing near our dressing room door waiting to see my counterpart Albert. I thought it was my lucky day as he handed me his shirt but he just told me to give it to Filipe Teixeira, who was a friend of his from the Portuguese team. Never mind. Talking of big hitters, one of the strangest sights we had was of Jose Mourinho occupying the chair used by the Hawthorns doorman, Joe, in the passage for virtually all of the pre-match. Perhaps he was exhausted after watching the Chelsea team coach being unloaded. They once turned up at our place with 11 skips and three massage beds. It was still very much us and them and, in terms of our bid for consolidation on the pitch, we never recovered from a poor start that included a Carling Cup defeat at Hartlepool.

With nothing like that much gear to haul around, we must have had too much time on the overnight trips for cooking up ideas because, after the draw at Portsmouth in the April, just after Joe Corrigan had tipped me off that he would be leaving at the end of the season, we decided to wind Mark Venus up. Peter Grant was also in on the plot to tell Veno the police wished to speak to him because he had been mouthing off to the fourth official during the game. He rushed his shower and scrambled into his clothes before returning with a puzzled look and to the sight of us doubled up. That's when he realised he had been had. Big Joe didn't just leave me with memories of his dry sense of humour. He also gave me a signed pair of his gloves when he departed.

I had a relaxed relationship with Tony Mowbray. He let me disappear with Del the masseur for a couple of hours the night before the game at Blackburn on the last day of the season. We went for a game of bowls with the Blackburn kit-man Alan, who was looking forward to his final match after learning of a generous whip-round among the players by way of a leaving present. I had a good understanding with most of my counterparts around the country and remember being disappointed that Alex at Middlesbrough had lost his job after we flew there for a League game early in 2009-10. Knowing he wasn't as enamoured with the club as he had been, I asked him in a text: "Do you want us to give them a good stuffing for you today?" I sent him another message after the game, saying: "Was that okay?" We had won 5-0. He was chuffed.

Tony was always supportive of me and, when he and Mark Venus left for pastures new in Scotland in 2009, told me he would bring Celtic down for a game if the club were to grant me a testimonial. Some would say I was overdue one. Even when I had my photo taken with the 1978-79 team at Tony Godden's testimonial in the mid-1980s, the players couldn't believe I'd had not had a match to mark my 25-plus years. It was suggested to Sid Lucas then that I might be presented with a watch, to which he replied: "He already has one. Why does he need another?" Eventually, I got my watch after 35 years. Alan Buckley presented it to me at an end-of-season do and I still have the photo. I have frequently been asked why I haven't had a testimonial and don't really have an answer. I recall Dean Kiely and Neil Clement quizzing me about it early in Tony's reign, by which time I had clocked up more than 45 years. I even had thoughts of engaging the name of Sir Bobby Robson to help me get one. He had been a hero of mine as a youngster and, when I went to see Darren Eales to explore the possibility of a match, I explained that I would share the proceeds with Sir Bobby's Cancer Foundation if it came off. I became more aware of the organisation after I saw Sir Bobby for the last time. We were playing at Newcastle and he was having a meal upstairs. He had gone to the game because it was Albion. Joe Corrigan went up with me to see him and I took a poster for him to sign but I couldn't bring myself to ask him when I saw him in his wheelchair. I had got him an Albion shirt, signed by a few players, for his office, and just speaking to him meant more to me than any autograph.

Tony Mowbray had always been kind in indulging my sense of humour. Knowing he was a chocaholic, as was Michael Appleton, I used to give him a little treat, especially if we had lost and I thought he needed a lift. He was usually last on the coach home because of his interview duties and that gave me time to slip a Mars bar or Galaxy under the match programme or newspaper on his seat. My wife used to wonder why I disappeared while we were in the supermarket. It was the nearest Tony has to a vice and he never spoke about it publicly but I'd quietly ask later if he had enjoyed his guilty pleasure. He and Mark Venus entered a draw once at The Village Hotel in Walsall and won a fridge. They decided it was going in the staff room to keep the chocolate bars in. One Christmas, I wrapped sprouts in Ferrero Rocher wrapping paper for him and, when he and his staff left after our relegation in 2009 and they asked me to send their boots on, I couldn't resist having one final bit of mischief at their expense. I put a bar of Cadbury's fruit and nut in Tony's, a betting slip in Veno's with the words '£1,000 to win the League and Cup double' and some shortbread for their third-in-command, Peter Grant. They wouldn't have expected anything less.

Chapter Twenty Two

Tastes Like Team Spirit

Thank goodness there's good footage – a special dvd even – of our famous win at Old Trafford in December, 1978. I swear I was pissed at the game and didn't see events unfold very clearly. Because it was a bitterly cold day, with snow in the air, Ron Atkinson had decided we would have a tipple on the bench every time a goal went in. It finished Manchester United 3 Albion 5, so I was well gone by the end. Big Ron liked his Chivas Regal and maybe our intake that afternoon partly explained why he went into our dressing room at half-time and gave a rousing team talk to the effect: "Lads, you're playing brilliantly. Just keep knocking it around and that equaliser will come." When someone piped up and said it was 3-3 because Bomber had equalised in the dying seconds of the half, he changed tack to: "Well, just keep pinging it around and we'll soon be in front." We had half an hour or so sobering up before Laurie and Cyrille scored in the last 15 minutes and the blurriness returned.

Here's a confession....the drinking wasn't a one-off, although that extent of indulgence was. For decades, we had a tipple at matches – a little something before kick-off or in the dug-out during the game. It began either in Don Howe's time or Johnny Giles's first spell, with George Wright seeing to it that we had a little 'warmer' in a hip flask. The habit meant there was one extra item on that skip check-list I was writing about. Certainly, it was Don who introduced me to George's favourite tipple, Glenfiddich, in the Royal Garden Hotel in Kensington, which we used for years before games in London. I couldn't afford a bottle for myself but was happy to join in if the club were providing them, as they did in those days. Ron Wylie loved malt whisky and complained when I turned up with only half a bottle. He ordered me to ask

Dennis Lewis, who was in charge of the directors' suite on a match day, for a top-up and to get a bottle of brandy while I was at it. He always wanted a full bottle, so I used to collect the leftovers and recycle them or take them home as Christmas presents. We never finished a bottle.

It was more than a cold-weather thing, although you might have two nips on a winter's day. We called the practice 'team spirit' and most of the managers happily went along with it because they didn't want to break the tradition. Gary Megson liked his brandy, so that was always packed in the skip and the players would never see it. They were out on the pitch warming up when the glasses came out and the tell-tale signs had been removed by the time the lads came back in. Actually, that's not 100 per cent true. On one freezing day at Port Vale before Gary's time, Paul Peschisolido was persuaded to have a sip because the whisky that day was Canadian. Then he went out and scored twice! Gary used to reckon we looked like Real Madrid after he had had a few sips. Frank Burrows and the club chaplain Ken Hipkiss would be at it as well. A bit later, Nigel Pearson used to put a warmer in the Lucozade bottle he carried with him. Gary Shelton, one of our coaches a decade or so ago, liked it and we had some fun at his expense by doing him a cold, weak tea which looked like whisky. He spat it out the second it passed his lips. Gary spat some out once as well because it was Martell, not Courvoisier. There's sophistication for you!

We used to see the opposition at it as well....West Ham spring to mind. But Tony Mowbray didn't participate. He just didn't like alcohol, not even wine. He never acquired the taste after it made him sick as a youngster. On the overnight trips, he would always get a round in at the bar for his staff after dinner and knock back something like a J2O, possibly as we had a quiz. Then he would be first off to bed. But his successor Roberto Di Matteo had a drink before games with Derrick the masseur and Dr Rimmer. Occasionally the Doc's daughter, Judith, would join in a few years earlier. Laurie Rampling, the club's jovial and loyal photographer, was another who thought it was rude to say no. In nearly all weathers, he would be there in his shorts as we cosied up – in the dressing room if it was an away game or in the tunnel area at The Hawthorns. Sometimes I'd have the drinks poured before they appeared and it was like Santa's mince pies. I'd return from doing one or two jobs and the goodies would be gone. One of the non-playing players got there first once and had himself something he obviously preferred to tea.

Robbie might have more than one, especially when the pressure was on, so I used to leave him a re-fill for half-time. It was done discreetly and not blatantly in front of the players. It wasn't the only vice supporters might not be aware of. Robbie also liked a smoke and always asked a member of staff to usher him to a safe area after games, so he could light up without any accusing looks. His assistant, Eddie Newton, had a ritual of his own. He is a Muslim and used to get out his prayer mat, or at least a towel, before games. At The Hawthorns, it would be in one of the back rooms off the dressing room. He'd do it just as the team went out and pray for a few minutes. I would leave him and wait to pack the rest of the stuff up. It wasn't unknown for him to miss a kick-off.

At the same time, I would be gathering in the warm-up kit, sweeping round with the brush, getting spare boots collected or whatever....all those jobs I could get on better with when the place was empty. We also used to save the tie-ups at the more frugal end of the Sid Lucas's era, so picking those up ready for washing and re-using was another task. Now they are routinely thrown away. I missed most of a match at Gillingham early in the new Millennium because there was dirty water or sewage coming up the drains. My assistant Andy and I took it in turns to stay with the workmen and keep the door open to get rid of the smell in the tiny dressing rooms. I can't say my appetite was the best after the fitness coach Adie Stovell had cooked the microwave meals for the return journey but at least we won 2-1, so the day wasn't a complete ordeal.

Relegation in 2009 brought cutbacks and I lost my assistant, Mark Gascoigne. Bamber was made redundant around the time we were welcoming Roberto and a backroom team that included Ade Mafe as well as Eddie Newton. At least Bamber had something to fall back on as he ran his own car valeting service. My workload increased considerably and, before we found ourselves on the same plane as Leicester when we flew out of Stansted for our pre-season tour of Slovenia, I had lots to pack. Along with the usual ton of match kit and training gear, each player had two tracksuits, two zip poly black polos, two zip poly silver polos, one black cotton buttoned top and one silver cotton buttoned top. I was devastated on the first full day of the tour when I heard John Hartson had been diagnosed with cancer of the brain. I could have cried and felt so inadequate in sending him a text reading: "Oh, John boy. I am so sorry to hear the news. Stay strong. You are a winner. You can and will win this battle. God bless." We were getting information through Craig Beattie and some of it, like the suggestion he may have only 72 hours to live, was very alarming. Most of my memories of him are happy ones. We were playing Swansea a few years ago when he went to their changing room for a chat with a couple of players he knew and the mascot was outside waiting for his big moment – the chance to walk out with the teams. The little lad recognised John and was given a tenner by him for knowing who he was. I texted John several times during his battle and told him to stay strong.

It wasn't the only bad news at that time. On the last day of July, Clare phoned me to say Sir Bobby Robson – one of the icons of the English game for decades, let alone a hero from my early years at The Hawthorns – had died. It wasn't a very happy time. It had been seriously hot when we were in Slovenia a couple of years earlier – it was 39 degrees in the shade then apparently and the kick-off against Red Star Belgrade had to be put back as a result. That made it very different from when we faced them in the UEFA Cup in 1979 on what was a bitterly cold trip. Now this 2009 tour took place under a cloud of a different kind. Adrian Chiles turned up for dinner one night but any glimpse of him or any other member of our celebrity supporter set provided only temporary respite. It was a tough period. The laundry burned down soon after our return and I had to make sure dear old Mo had a chair and drink when I broke the news to her and her assistant Lyn on their arrival that day. We knew they would take it badly. We suspected an electrical fault but I learned later that Arsenal and Crystal Palace had had similar incidents and it was felt that the massage oils on the towels might have played a part. I brought loads of kit home for Carol and our neighbour Margaret to wash. It must have been an eye-opener for the other neighbours. I swear it was the first and only time I've taken a photo of Margaret's washing line.

As if that extra workload wasn't enough over the next two or three weeks, I had a call to say a fire had broken out in the meantime at Easy Clean, the place that took some of the burden off us after our blaze. We lost training kit and some schoolboys' bags. The stress of the additional work, coming on top of losing Bamber, caught up with me and I think I made more mistakes for an early-season trip to Bury than I had for any game in the previous 48 years. I forgot new signing Joe Mattock's boots, some red skins, flip-flops, the tactics board, and blood shirts and shorts. It wasn't a happy day. My nerves weren't helped when we went to Nottingham Forest the following weekend and the fire alarms went off. I was probably half-way up the floodlight pylons before being told it was a false alarm. I worked 52 hours one week and made it clear I wasn't going to do more than the maximum of 48. Everything seemed difficult. I had to battle for 12 months to have two shelves and a rail for the bench coats fitted in the kit room. There was talk of an assistant coming in after the turn of the year and I found I needed my sense of humour more than ever. When Robbie noticed me handing out cakes for the staff to celebrate my birthday, I said: "I was 63 yesterday." He answered: "Oh, happy 63rd birthday for yesterday." He looked puzzled when I came back with: "No, I was 63 yesterday. I'm 64 today." Many of the staff had heard it before.

Roberto's first competitive game in charge, at home to Newcastle in August, 2009, had been a sad one. It was just after Sir Bobby Robson's passing and there was an impressive line-up of former players on the edge of the pitch for the minute's applause in his honour. I saw Don Howe at the ground for the first time since he had been manager here and got him to sign the shirt he gave me in 1961 to start my collection. Also there for an occasion that moved supporters of both clubs were Derek Kevan, Roy Horobin, Brian Whitehouse, Stan Jones, Alec Jackson, Chuck Drury, Keith Smith, Dave Burnside, Graham Williams, Brian Macready and Stuart Williams. I was glad I had made the effort to go and see Sir Bobby when I last had the chance. Davey Burnside, one of his closest friends, died suddenly a few weeks later at a time when he was hoping to become an MP for the UKIP party and when he was also writing his autobiography.

We started well on the pitch and were soon up among the pacesetters. Youssouf Mulumbu had come into the side after being signed during Tony's reign and we won five games in a row after drawing with Newcastle. No-one could deny that we had the knack of winning promotion and it quickly looked like we would be challenging strongly again. Robbie kept things interesting by arranging a warm-weather trip to Spain in the November. Dan Ashworth turned up and, as is the 'norm' on such occasions, a buzz went round the camp as to whether he had been sent out as a spy by the chairman. Team-wise, our progress was all very smooth, which was in marked contrast to when we touched down back on English soil. The landing was the worst I've ever known and was nearly aborted because of the high winds that were buffeting us. I was sitting close to the emergency exit and found myself reading the safety instructions even more carefully at the end of that flight than at the start of it.

There were still problems off the field, notably with the laundry area being that cold in the winter that poor Mo had to work with her coat on, but the club were doing a lot right as well. We had come so far since the days when we considered staying in what is now known as the Championship to be more of a priority than trying to climb out of it. We were heading towards promotion again and I was proud to be part of it. My service was into its 50th year when we celebrated at Doncaster after reaching the Premier League once more. Robbie was the 25th manager I had worked for – that's just the permanent ones, not the caretakers – and my stint dwarfed even guys like Vic Akers, who worked for Arsenal for decades and as manager of their highly successful women's team, and the long-serving Roy Reyland at Tottenham. Mind you, I have to confess here: I did miss a couple of Albion games in the 21st century when we flew to Scotland for a couple of family weddings in Banff. The first of them was for Carol's cousin's son Ian, who I used to take miniature Albion kits for when I was up there either with the club or the family. I think that was the first time I had been absent from a League or cup game for approaching 20 years since I had suffered for around ten days from a really bad stomach bug and couldn't get out of bed. The other happy event surrounded Carol's cousin's daughter Kay at the start of March several years ago. I was obviously badly missed. On the first occasion, we thrashed Manchester City 4-0. The second time, we beat Plymouth 3-0.

Chapter Twenty Three

A Strange Thing Happened

You wouldn't believe what an eerie place a football ground is towards midnight. Many's the time I've had to lock up following an evening fixture because I've been the last one still working there. I was transfixed in the dead of one night by something creeping over towards me on the pitch. There wasn't a soul about and I was convinced it was a fox because I thought I could see the light of its eyes. There was a rustling every now and again and I had a chuckle when this scary 'creature' arrived at my feet. It was a bloody crisp packet. Late nights and Christmas duties were the bane of my working life, I suppose. I never put off until the morning what really needed to be done in the late hours – just in case there was bad weather the next day, or I was ill. Or the manager announced a change of routine that may have thrown me. I had to be professional. Working on Christmas Day most years was obviously a down-side. I would often leave just after lunch if we were away on Boxing Day and therefore staying overnight. If we were at home, I'd go in early enough as to be home for lunch with the family. The arrangements would be the same around New Year, although I was generally spared having to join the squad if the manager insisted on having them together in a local hotel to keep them out of temptation's way before a home game.

On a much lighter note, a strip-o-gram was organised for me when the players had a whip-round to help me celebrate my 40 years' service. Normally, I keep my eyes very much on the ball at work but, on this occasion, they obviously wandered slightly because I recorded in my diary: "She was dressed as a policewoman and was flat-chested." As Brian Jensen wrote in his column in the Sporting Star: "She wasn't a stunner." I was sufficiently emboldened to say to the lads afterwards: "Obviously, a buxom, better-looking girl would have cost more. Typical of the club to do it on the cheap." Albion presented me with a cake bearing the club crest and three pages were dedicated in the programme to a feature about me. I couldn't resist the temptation to point out to Gary Megson that he was given only one page for his column. I also did a piece for John Simpson (now in charge of the club's media department) in the Evening Mail, and the Sports Argus and Birmingham Post ran their own features. John and the club's programme editor Dave Bowler both used the milestone to suggest I did a book, so I told them I already had one in mind. To complete a busy few days, the supporters asked me to do something on video that they could show on the coaches to forthcoming away games.

I hope this publication has contained a few humorous asides but a few more of them can be grouped together here as they didn't seem to fit naturally anywhere else. And you'll see that I had to be prepared to be the butt of the dressing room humour on occasions. At training on one of the overnight stays in Durham, I was joined by my assistant Bamber behind the goal to stop the balls disappearing into a river. Our efforts were a bit of a side show at first but became the main attraction when the staff did some shooting practice at the end and deliberately had us scrambling about on the bank. They thought it was hilarious. The joke was on me again when I soaked myself at Watford while manoeuvring the skip into the shower area. I backed into the shower handle and turned it on. Another time, before a local game, we were to stay at the Village Hotel in Dudley and Gary told me to pack the under-13 kit. I was utterly perplexed but it was his way of lightening the mood at a tense time and making the lads more relaxed. They weren't too impressed at first but eventually Ruel Fox twigged......it was all done for a laugh. Darren Moore looked like he was wearing a blue and white striped boob tube and white Speedos as the lads did a warm-up session in their miniature kit on the grass by the road, attracting some very strange looks from motorists as they did so.

I once went without James Chambers' shirt to a game at Manchester City because no-one had told me he was in the squad. I had to have his name stitched on at their club shop, although he wasn't required in the end. James also wanted a new sock in a game at Walsall. I thought he might have muddled by – there were only five minutes to go before half-time. If I thought I had my work cut out at times, I found out from the Huddersfield kit-man, who was only a young lad, that they used to take a player's name off a shirt when he left and stitched the name of a replacement on; all to save money obviously. We once had a lad among our substitutes with no proper number on his shirt. Gary Megson was relaxed about it. He said he wouldn't go on anyway. It was a cup game and the youngster sat on the bench with someone else's shirt on and nobody was any the wiser. It was a rare case of making do because, by now, we were entering the era in which everything was done for footballers. It was a bit different in the 1960s, when the players had two pairs of boots and a pair of rubbers for training. They fetched them themselves from sports shops by handing in vouchers provided by the club. Also provided for them were two white training tops, two pairs of shorts and socks and two lots of underwear (briefs or jock straps) – and very little else.

The increase in the size of our match-day entourage caught up with me at Norwich once. There wasn't room for me on the bench and there were no spare seats round about, so, when I was told by a jobsworth that I couldn't stand in the tunnel, I went and waited in the dressing room. I had a strop on but found some jobs to do. What was it about East Anglia? Three years running, I got locked in at Ipswich. It was quite a walk from the dressing room to the pitch and there was a door which someone had locked without checking we were all out. I had a right moan at him and the following year, I swear he locked me in on purpose out of revenge. Tony Mowbray recently reminded me of the time he was playing against us at Portman Road and two of our players lost their cool following a defeat to such an extent that they swung a few blows at each other in the tunnel. A steward was caught in the crossfire and it was agreed we should send compensation to him because of his slight injuries. That should have been the end of it. Trouble was, we sent it to Norwich rather than Ipswich.

Chapter Twenty Four

An All-Too-Brief Time With Roy

I would love to have spent more time working with Roy Hodgson. His playing career was quite modest but he had been a big success as a manager in several countries and that guaranteed respect. The players wanted to listen to him because of what he had achieved in the game. Tony Mowbray used to say you needed a squad to buy into the story you were trying to write and buy into the game plan every match day. Like him, Roy was not one for ranting and raving and I could relate to his ideas for togetherness. Bernard McNally moaned to me once about what Bobby Gould was asking the squad to do and I told him to go and see him to discuss it because if we had players chipping away and not taking on what the manager was asking, we had no chance. He emerged from Gouldy's office to say: "Well, that's made a difference. He's dropped me!"

Roy took over when Robbie Di Matteo was sacked in the February of our first season back up and steered us to a position well out of danger. In the March, the Supporters Club kindly organised a 50th anniversary dinner for me and I was thrilled and humbled at the turn-out of ex-players and staff........Alec Jackson, Brian Whitehouse, Stan Jones, Graham Williams, Bobby Hope, John Kaye, Micky Fudge, Tony Brown, Ray Wilson, Alistair Robertson, John Wile, Bobby Gould, Alistair Brown, Joe Mayo, John Trewick, Derek Statham, Cyrille Regis, Derek Monaghan, Nicky Cross, Brendon Batson, Gary Robson, Don Goodman, Craig Shakespeare, Daryl Burgess, Paul Raven, Gary Strodder, Ian Hamilton, Bob Taylor, Richard Sneekes, Darren Moore, Michael Appleton, Dean Kiely, Lee Hughes, Neil Clement, Albert McPherson, Johnny Giles, Ron Atkinson, Colin Addison, Brian Talbot, Ossie Ardiles, Keith Burkinshaw, Tony Mowbray and Roy Hodgson. I was asked to name what I considered to be the best 11 Albion players from my 50 years and plumped for this magnificent line-up in a 4-3-3 formation: Osborne; Howe, Wile, Kaye, Statham; Tony Brown, Bryan Robson, Giles; Cunningham, Astle, Johnston. With Roy Hodgson listening with interest and my boss at the time, I chose him as the best manager. I'm not daft.

My selection caused some great banter with Alistair Robertson, who I knew well enough from old times to still refer to him in our phone conversations and texts as a ginger git. His hair isn't quite that colouring but I see enough of Billy Connolly in him due to their accents to ensure the name has somehow stuck. It's nothing to what he calls me. Around once a month, he texts me with the remark: "How are you, you old bastard?" It gave him even more ammunition when he was (just) overlooked in my best all-time Albion XI and he ribbed me by pointing out that the people who really understand the game, the supporters, had selected him in their best XI and that was all that mattered to him. At the dinner, there was a display of letters from various Premier League managers expressing their congratulations. One was from Sir Alex Ferguson, who I had had my picture taken with in Tony Mowbray's office not long before. He said it was a case of the longest-serving kit-man being photographed with the longest-serving manager. Among the items I was presented with that night was a bottle of whisky, which is still unopened and with a label bearing the message: 'Dave Matthews, 50 Years of Service, Look Back and Smile.' From Albion, there was a lovely lead crystal decanter and glasses.

That spring was pretty much the extent of my day-to-day duties with Roy Hodgson. After the Everton home game and before we went to Newcastle for our final match of the season, we had the Monday off and I was in the shower when I felt a lump the size of a small egg in my neck. I didn't want to worry Carol by telling her but decided to see the club doctor Kevin Conod the following day. We went into a private room off the players' treatment room and I sat down so he could press round my stomach area. His words were: "This needs investigating. We can't ignore it. We will get you into Little Aston to have an endoscopy (a look inside my body via camera)." I had to let Carol know then – she works at my doctor's anyway. We were in training on the Saturday before going to Newcastle and Kev rang me at 9am and said: "Thank God it's not stomach cancer." That was his main concern, although I didn't know it. But he told me it still needed further looking at. At St James', we were so poor in the first half that we were three down at the interval. I was distracted and looking for jobs to do in the dressing room rather than too concerned with the game. The fightback came in the second half and we salvaged a point but, as our goals went in, I didn't want to go out and risk breaking the side's luck, so I carried on packing.

I informed Roy Hodgson about the lump and he told me to do what I needed to do. There were precious few symptoms. My stomach glands were swollen and I joked about it being my six-pack. It's a defence mechanism that I made light of it. I was back in Little Aston a few days after the game and a biopsy revealed it was lymphoma. They told me if you had to choose a cancer, this would be one to have because the success rate with it was high. They told me I'd have to have chemotherapy and I went to the Manor Hospital in Walsall on the NHS. One of the nurses said they couldn't believe how relaxed I was. I just took it in my stride. I knew I had to go through the course but I knew I would be going back to work and my outlook was positive. I had no negativity.

Derrick Jones, the club masseur, took me when I first had the camera down inside me and also accompanied me on at least one other hospital visit. We were good mates. He lived two minutes away in Halesowen and used to walk over the fields with his dogs – a Labrador, Jack Russell and a cross-breed of some kind – to see us. He and his wife and daughter-in-law ran a clinic in Blackheath and Kevin Campbell said he was the best masseur he knew. I would give Derrick two t-shirts for a match day. He couldn't wear the one for the game that he had on beforehand because he was so vigorous in his work that he sweated a lot and had to wring it out. He had joined the club towards the end of the Gary Megson era in succession to two females, one of whom gave me a massage once when I had a bad back. They were nice looking girls but Gary wasn't happy with them. Derrick had gone all over the world laying pipes and could have been a clay pigeon shooter for England as well as being involved in amateur dramatics and learning to sing. He was a talented guy. Would you believe, he was also diagnosed with cancer and I returned the favour by running him to hospital. Sadly, his illness was more acute than mine and he didn't recover. The football side of the club shut down on the day of his funeral, where the turn-out was predictably large. His wife Marion asked me recently if I'd like his bowls. We used to play at Somers, a council-run club where I've been a member for a long while, although I couldn't play during my illness. I was looking forward to spending some time with Derrick in my retirement and this beautiful set of bowls is the next best thing. I miss him a lot.

Because I had no other medical problems, the medical people were going to hit me hard with the chemo. I had a trial dose and stayed overnight in case of a reaction. There was none, so my first proper dose the next day lasted five hours. I stayed over again and was fine but they couldn't discharge me as my records went astray. It turned out my specialist had taken my notes to a meeting, so I had to stay in for the weekend. I didn't mind because I had never been hospitalised before and I was the most mobile of the five blokes in the ward. I became a bit of a gofer and it opened my eyes to a few things. I had chemo every 21 days and had my temperature taken several times per visit. Running a temperature was something I had to be careful of, so I declined the club's request to go to a game. I had to be very careful of mixing with crowds, not knowing whether the person next to me had a cold or cough. I was in hospital for five days at one point and visitors had to come in wearing masks and gowns. Only once did I feel really rough. Otherwise, the biggest problem was that my voice went up a few octaves.

At home, I had an interesting keepsake at my side as I spent hours and hours in the summer house which we'd had built a couple of months before I was taken ill. On an overseas club trip, I had been told to pack in the skip a huge cow bell we had been given by our hosts. We kept it at the ground and Ron Atkinson told me to ring it before one match because he sensed the players were too quiet. Brendon Batson told me to sod off but Ron said: "Ignore him, keep ringing it. Upset them." We won. When Ron came back a year or two later with United, I clanged it in the corridor outside their dressing room and checked my watch to see how long it was before he came out to see me. It was about ten seconds. He offered me £50 for it and I held out for £100, so the bell was still in my kit room during Tony Mowbray's time and came in useful during my recuperation when I needed Carol. I had no energy for walking round much and have to say I enjoyed, for a short time, being waited on hand and foot. I was lucky with the side effects to my illness and the worst I had was constipation. As with my squeaky voice, though, the problem was addressed through the counter-balancing of my medication once I told the staff. I also lost my hair and eye lashes. They all came back after a few months but not before Chris Kirkland failed to recognise me in the tunnel at Wigan. He apologised. The girls were obviously concerned but relieved it wasn't stomach cancer. There were no tears that I'm aware of, not in my presence anyway and definitely not by me. I kept reminding myself and others that I had had a lovely life but had always been blessed with optimism anyway and was convinced I would survive even if I was ever in a plane crash.

I didn't want to retire. I was enjoying the job and getting on well with Roy. I like to think I got on with all the managers. If I hadn't had health problems, I would still probably have been there now. Roy and his staff were good with me. He was old school and there's nothing wrong with that. He had lived in an era when money was much tighter and he appreciated what you did. He talks sense and simplicity, so why would the players not perform for him? I'd like to have been with him much longer than I was. He wasn't flash in any way. He liked quality and enjoyed good food and a glass of red, although the 'team spirit' thing was not really for him. He never said he didn't like us doing it, though, so we'd have a quiet tipple while his players were out warming up.

I had seven sessions of chemo and my scans revealed some little white specks – protein produced by my body – which they wanted to keep an eye on. Things took another turn and I realised something was wrong when I came to the end of my chemo and started my walking regime at the Manor Hospital in Walsall. Instead of my work-outs becoming longer and easier, they were getting shorter and harder and I found myself out of breath even just going upstairs. My doctor sent me for an x-ray and I had fluid on my lungs, so I was put on tablets, which did the trick. I had to go to London to the Royal Free Hospital and what they thought was speckling was in fact amyloidosis – protein latching on to an organ. In my case, it was my heart that was being affected and the protein can harden and stop the organ working properly. The Royal Free is the only hospital in the country specialising in this condition. I had a heart biopsy and was more concerned by this development than the cancer. It took three months for the results to come through and they were good news because I had the better of the two types of amyloidosis. They said at the hospital they would try to slow or stop the protein forming but they couldn't reverse the process.

This was the diagnosis behind my retirement. The club wanted to know what was happening as they had engaged Pat Frost, a former England kit-man and a home and away Albion supporter. I had met him in Holland on one of our pre-season trips, when he drove there with his kids despite having come back from the World Cup in South Africa only a few days earlier. The club were keeping him on until Christmas and Roy was happy with him, although he knew I had wanted to go back. He said he hoped the two of us could work together and one plan was for Pat to do the away games and tours and I'd basically help at home games and maybe do the reserves. I said I thought the club should extend Pat's contract and I'd go back as assistant kit-man. But the biopsy result made me think again. I retired in May, 2012 – well into my 51st year at the club, although I didn't work any of it. I went in and Mo the laundry lady was the first person I told of my decision. It upset her. Then I informed Roy before going in to see the secretary Richard Garlick. As I was coming out, the chairman was around and asked me how I was. I said I was doing okay. I was flattered when Pat Frost told me it was the hardest job in the world following me. I told him to forget me and just do it his way. I didn't have much strength and couldn't have lifted the skip on to the coach any more because there had been wastage of my muscles. It was time to go and time for some more reflection and to finish my autobiography at last.

There was plenty to write because of all the changes I had seen unfold! Derek Kevan, Bobby Robson and Don Howe were among the big noises when I had been appointed, players wore one to 11 and the arrival of a Welshman or Scotsman in the dressing room was about as cosmopolitan or exotic as the game was. Now, we had a huge backroom staff, foreigners galore, millionaire players and seven substitutes. I had seen and enjoyed so much and wouldn't have missed it for the world. There were some brilliant memories to sustain me and I had no shortage of moral support during my treatment. We had known other cancer sufferers at the club like Geoff Horsfield, John Hartson and Frank Burrows, and Bryan Robson was diagnosed after he left us for the second time. All had recovered well. I was thrilled John pulled through because he seemed to be in a bad way and is a likeable character with plenty to offer. He had left by the time I had my diagnosis and, having lost all the numbers in my phone, I managed to re-contact him through Suzan, the kit-lady at Swansea. During my rehabilitation, she very kindly sent some Welsh cakes, which Derrick Jones and I ate in my summer house.

I had good-luck texts from work colleagues or counterparts such as Dennis Butler at Birmingham and Andy at Milton Keynes. I knew him through Roberto

Di Matteo, who had worked at the MK Dons before coming to Albion. The kind gestures continued. Gary Megson, then manager of Sheffield Wednesday, invited me as his guest for their match at Walsall. I thanked him but declined, saying it just missed out on the opportunity to go and watch Albion v Manchester City. I also had an approach that might conceivably have made me a very regular visitor to the Banks's Stadium. Richard O'Kelly was trying to get me to go to there as the Saddlers' kit-man, although I'm not sure there would have been any pay. At the same time, I did well with invites from kit suppliers. Returning some of the goodwill, I texted Roy Hodgson when we beat Sweden at the European Championships. I said he had broken a few bogeys at Albion by winning at Villa, Stoke and Liverpool – now he had done it with England as well. He took the trouble to reply, as he always does. When I used to text him after Albion wins, he'd say: "Keep a good thing going… ….don't break the run now." If we lost, I'd say something like: "Right, time to go off on another run." One of his favourite sayings was: "There are two teams at a football club; one on the pitch, one off it."

At my retirement do in the Millichip Suite at The Hawthorns in the spring of 2012, about 100 friends and colleagues, past and present, came along. I received a tankard from Albion honouring my 'lifelong service.' They also gave me a nice cheque. I said my farewells to the existing staff at that game against Arsenal and sat in the dug-out for the last time at what was also Roy's last game with us. Not long afterwards, Alison and I sat down together to watch the 2002 promotion winners' dvd and remind ourselves of the drama and history we had lived through ten years earlier. Then again, there had been so many dramas. As an Albion fan, I had been very, very lucky to experience the long working life I had.

Chapter Twenty Five

A Happy Life Celebrated

You could forgive Albion fans for dreading games against Newcastle.
It was at the Magpies' visit to The Hawthorns in August, 2009 that
supporters of both clubs mourned the passing of Sir Bobby Robson. The trip
to St James' Park on the last day of the 2010-11 season was Dave Matthews'
last hands-on match day in the Albion dressing room and, on the afternoon of
Alan Pardew's side's visit to The Hawthorns on April 20, 2013, Carol
Matthews was joined on the touchline beneath the Halfords Lane Stand by
daughters Alison and Clare, and Dave's sister-in-law Chris Matthews – widow
of his late brother Frank – as a 25,671 crowd stood as one in the sunshine to
celebrate his life with a minute's applause. As if the moment wasn't emotional
enough, a picture of his smiling face showed on the big screen at the same
time.

A week earlier, with tickets provided by Alison, Dave had gone with Albion
Supporters Club chairman John Homer and vice-chairman Dave Holloway to
the Wolves v Huddersfield game. They had tea and sandwiches in the Bert
Williams Lounge beforehand and, fun-loving to the end, Dave had seen a
photograph of Alistair Robertson in the programme and texted the veteran
defender with a suitably mischievous comment, probably concerning the fact
that he was wearing a gold shirt. He also exchanged pleasantries with
Huddersfield's goalkeeper coach Paul Crichton, the Baggies' last line of
defence for a season or two in the second half of the 1990s. So much did the
trio enjoy their day out in the Championship that they planned to go back to
Wolves' home game against promotion-bound Hull on the Tuesday. Dave
Holloway, of Baggies Travel fame, was heard to say: "As an Albion fan, you
want to hate the Wolves really. But we were well looked after, we had a lovely

day and decided that we would go back in the week." Tragically, in the meantime, Dave Matthews, having tended to some of the other loves of his life by cutting his lawns and enjoying the normal Sunday family lunch in the company of neighbours Margaret and Betty, passed away at home while watching Match of the Day 2. Crichton had thus become the last Albion player the veteran kit-man saw out of the thousands he knew.

By one of those strange quirks, Alison had left her parents' house on that Sunday night and driven home to catch some of The Shawshank Redemption just before going to bed and then receiving the sort of phone call everybody dreads. What's strange is that her dad was much too restless to enjoy films – he never sat down and watched them – but had returned from one of his later Albion away days enthusing over a film he had seen on the team coach. It was, of course, The Shawshank Redemption.

Dave's last trip to Albion had been for Arsenal's visit on April 6, when he and Carol were guests of Lucozade. It was another occasion for some socialising as well as for viewing a game from a good seat high in the stand rather than through a forest of legs from the dug-out. The couple enjoyed a pre-match meal and Dave, as the only one of the two carrying money, paid for the bet Carol placed on the Gunners leading both at half-time and full-time. He collected her £15 winnings, handed it to her and, in return, received the stake back. The club's photographer Laurie Rampling witnessed this scant consolation on a day of Baggies disappointment and captured the moment in his time-honoured way from behind the lens. "In lieu of the 'team spirit' moments we had shared at so many grounds up and down the country, Dave very kindly bought me a miniature bottle of Jameson Irish Whiskey to toast their good fortune," Laurie said. "He knew I like my malt but I can't bring myself to drink it. It's still on display on the bookcase at home." The bottle was passed on to Laurie by Ally Robertson, who had been on corporate duty at the game with Joe Mayo and Stewart Woolgar – the latter a goal-scoring member of Albion's FA Youth Cup final side of 1969. In addition to being the visitors for Dave's last match-day appearance at the ground, Arsenal had also been the opponents for his final game before retirement the previous spring; the one played at the end of a season in which he was absent throughout.

There was huge sadness at the news of his passing. At home to Manchester United in the first game of the 2011-12 season the best part of two years earlier,

Jonas Olsson had organised Albion's players to wear warm-up shirts with the message 'Get well soon, Dave' on the backs. Clare's Facebook wall contains a picture of Gonzalo Jara Reyes spreading the message. After the awful announcement had come, Chris Brunt kicked off his captain's column in the following weekend's match programme by describing the retired kit-man as 'a proper club man who loved the Albion.' A two-page feature elsewhere in the magazine called him 'an extraordinary servant to the beautiful game, a truly great Albion man and a lovely fella to boot.' The article also referred to him as a doyen among kit-men. That day, in a draw against Newcastle, Steve Clarke's side wore the same black armbands that Dave would have carried in the skips a thousand times.

The guests in a huge turn-out at the funeral at St John the Baptist Church in Halesowen on Wednesday, May 1, represented an A to Z of the great and good of Albion's history over the last half a century; Addison, Batson, Ally Brown, Tony Brown, Brunt, Dave Butler, Cantello, Adam Chambers, James Chambers, Corrigan, Campbell Crawford, Nicky Cross, Cumbes, Donovan, Downing, Dyer, Eves, Fairfax, Fudge, Hamilton, Hartford, Hodgkisson, Horsfield, Hope, Stan Jones, Kiely, Mardon, Mayo, McPherson, Monaghan, Darren Moore, Morrison, Mowbray, O'Kelly, Olsson, Raven, Regis, Robertson, Bryan Robson, Gary Robson, Shakespeare, Talbot, Taylor, Venus, Whitehouse, Wile, Graham Williams. A guard of honour was in place in the warm sunshine for the lunchtime arrival of the coffin, which was carried by John Wile, Alistair Robertson, Bob Taylor, Cyrille Regis, Brendon Batson and Paul Raven.

Hartford, Cantello, Williams, Hope and the Robson brothers congregated in Wetherspoon's over the road from the church as they took some sustenance before the service and spoke of their great sadness. A cluster of Dave's counterparts from around the country gathered in the corner of the same room and then outside on the pavement as they chatted separately; Albert Morgan from Manchester United, Dennis Butler from Birmingham, two from Everton including the main man Jimmy Martin, Jim Paul's son Ian from Aston Villa and a representative from Arsenal. I asked around as to their length of service and even the most enduring of this loyal, long-serving group had barely made it half-way past Mr Albion's 50 years. "Nobody will do that again, it's an unbelievable length of time to survive in this game," was the consensus view.

They also agreed that joining in the dressing room banter was a good way of staying young.

Among the other guests were the Wolves secretary Richard Skirrow, who is Alison's boss, one-time Albion directors John Silk and Barry Hurst and two Hawthorns stalwarts in former secretary Dr John Evans and Dr Roger Rimmer. They heard another long-serving member of the Baggies 'family', club chaplain Ken Hipkiss, talk of a fresh-faced 15-year-old who basically knocked on the door in search of a job in 1960-61 and stayed around to serve 26 permanent managers and witness the winning of the FA Cup, the League Cup and six promotions. "He was only the second person in a non-playing capacity to win the Barclays Merit Award," he added, referring to the recognition that came nationally for his amazing service. Ken talked of a 'brilliant kit-man' in whom players and various staff members found a confidant, a solace and a shoulder to lean on; someone with whom secrets stuck. "He knew it wasn't his place to talk about the club in public and definitely not to slag anyone off," he said. "He was utterly discreet, kept his head down and had time for everybody. He genuinely cared for people. Once you met Dave, you remained his friend." Ken would well understand the importance of such qualities. He referred also to 'a calming influence, an encourager and someone who quietly went about his business in an often fierce dressing room." There was also a remark about how he had been recognised as 'Mr Albion' but the reverend had another name for him: Mr Constant.

The service included the hymn The Lord's My Shepherd, which Baggies fans sing with gusto when their team score, and a recital of a poem written by Dave's father Frank, and read by Alison. Also in attendance were a camera crew and various photographers. In the newspaper write-ups on the day, Bryan Robson, who started his career with the club in 1972, was quoted as saying: "I knew Dave when I was 13 years old when I started as a schoolboy. To us young lads, he was more or less the boss around the place. He was an unbelievable servant for the club. Seeing all the people here today, it just shows what a great kit manager he was. He was one of the best I ever knew. He was always supportive but, if you ever stepped out of line, he would tell you. He was great with people but he was a great disciplinarian as well." In a clip played that night on Central TV, physio Richie Rawlins spoke of Dave's kindness in helping him over his fear of planes by talking to him throughout a flight taking the squad on a pre-season tour. Following the service, a private family burial took place in Stourbridge and then there was a buffet and drinks at The Hawthorns, where flags had been flown at half mast.

Clare, who has become a regular Albion watcher again in the last year after following them home and away for many seasons from her mid teens, takes comfort from the fact that she moved back in with her parents in the early summer of 2012. As a result, she was able to spend a lot more time with him in his final year than would otherwise have been the case. They are not an overly sentimental family and speak openly about him as a way of coping with their grief. But she has also talked about enjoying sitting in the summer house at the top of the home's lovely garden since his passing as a way of feeling closer to him. Her father had died less than a year after retiring and almost two years on from his non-Hodgkin lymphoma diagnosis. It was while he had been having scans for the disease that he had been found to have his rare heart condition and the results of the post mortem, which came through around two months following his death, revealed him to have been clear of the cancer. He had evidently beaten it and the coroner's report concluded that the likelihood was that he had suffered an arrhythmia – a fatal problem with the rhythm or rate of the heartbeat.

Dave, typically, had pledged to take a table at the Supporters Club's 2002 promotion winners' reunion in early May. In the event, the places at the dinner, which was held only eight days after the funeral, were filled by Carol, Alison, myself, laundry lady Mo Brookes, who called Dave her 'work husband,' and Joe Davis. Doorman Joe, as he is known, was accompanied by his son and he himself did just over 49 years at The Hawthorns until his wife's ill health made it impossible for him to carry on. Long service inevitably pulled him close to Dave, who, just as he did with Laraine Astle, proved to be a rock. His instinct was to help friends in need, so he used to make regular trips to take Joe out for a pint in Oldbury.

Dave would have loved the banter of the reunion dinner. When interviewed on the mic by Supporters Club chairman John Homer, Michael Appleton and Derek McInnes in particular gave good insight into the mood engendered by Gary Megson – one the kit-man had much admired. Appleton revealed that he was signed by the manager not long after giving him a mouthful of abuse while being sent off for Preston in a reserve game against Albion. Clearly, Megson liked a feisty individual cut from the same cloth as himself. McInnes also testified to the mood his gaffer cultivated. "He absolutely ruled with fear but there was total respect," he said. "Everyone here would run through a brick wall for him – and probably still would." Remember what Dave had said about the need for togetherness behind a manager as far back as Bobby Gould's time in charge? It was a point he later reinforced within these pages when talking of the successful Tony Mowbray and Roy Hodgson eras.

Neil Reynolds, the chairman of Shareholders For Albion and a driving force behind the organisation's highly successful In Pastures Green book, was among the supporters to promise immediately to wear a retro shirt in Dave's memory for the visit of Manchester United on the last day of the season. One specially adapted top, showing a variety of designs of famous Albion shirts, read: "So many kits, but there's only one kit-man. RIP Dave Kit-Man Matthews." A month and a half later, a toast was raised to him at the former players' golf day at Walsall, where, as per the usual protocol, guests paused at dinner time to remember those who had been lost from the Albion family in the previous 12 months. The list also contained the names of Roy Horobin (one of Dave's work colleagues), Derek Kevan (one of his early heroes) and Tony Grealish.

Before we totally leave the subject of shirts, we should mention another project – the one Dave threw himself enthusiastically into while he was undergoing chemotherapy. He vowed to contact as many clubs and individuals as he could in search of signed shirts and, following the bumper response, sent off dozens and dozens of garments to be auctioned for Cancer Research. Many of them went under the hammer at the charity's Mistletoe Ball in London, where, as a further coincidence, one of them was bought by a work colleague of Clare's.

The story doesn't quite end there. The club's official photographer Laurie Rampling, whose expertise is reflected in some of the pictures in this book, thought he had retired from running marathons and half marathons, the last of his 236 such runs having been ground out in 2004. But he asked for the family's blessing in agreeing to hit the roads once more – in Dave's memory. His chosen event was this autumn's Birmingham Half Marathon, at which he ran in a shirt given to him by skipper Chris Brunt, who also saw to it that the dressing room led the sponsorship effort. Monies raised are going to UCL, a leading teaching and research university based in London. Another family friend took to the roads shortly before and raised several hundred pounds for amyloidosis research by competing in the Bournemouth Marathon – his first time over the distance.

Early this winter, Carol is going to visit her cousin Sandra from Willenhall, who now lives an hour or two from Perth in Western Australia. It is a trip she and Dave had planned to make together by using the Thomas Cook vouchers he had received as a leaving present from the players. She has now worked as a dispenser at her local doctor's for 32 years, having previously been on the payroll at Bannister and Thatcher in West Bromwich for 11. Alison was with Albion for more than 12 years prior to being made redundant and subsequently joining the backroom team at Wolves in 2005 and Clare has been employed for all of her 18 working years by the same law enforcement company in Birmingham. Her service and the time her mum has spent on her current payroll add up to another completed half a century and, apart from Carol leaving to start a family, none of the four has ever chosen to hand in their notice. Loyalty, long service and dependability are clearly qualities that run in the family.

Look back and smile.

In Memory of Dave

Maureen and Tom Adams
Colin Addison
Paul Ager
Franc Andrews
Nick Archer
Tom Ashfield
Claire Astle
Dawn Astle
Laraine Astle
Karl Aston
Charlotte Atkins
Ron Atkinson
Graham Avery
Lee Avery

John Albert Bailey
Paul Baker
Stuart Baker
Elaine Bannister
Elizabeth Bannister
Jan and Bill Barber
Jonathan Barber
Vincent Barber
Ian Barron
Margaret and Ian Barron
Dave Bassett
Liz and Rob Bate
In memory of Jeremy 'Jez' Bates
Matt, Deb, Lauren, Hannah
and Joe Batham
Brendon Batson MBE
Rob Batty
The Bayliss Family
Dave and Pat Beard
Paula Beardsmore
Derek and Christine Beasley
Tim Beech
Helen and Leigha Bench
Martyn Bennett
Simon Bennett
Trevor Bevan
Phil Birch
Duane Bishop
Gavin Blackwell
Mark Bott

Dave Bowen
Ashley Bradford
Kevin Bradford
Darren Bradley
Joe Bradley
Robert Bradley
Carl Brandrick
Joe Brandrick
Paul Bridges
Peter Brinton
Andrew Broadhurst
Nicky and Mike Brooke
Kay Brookes
Maureen Brookes 'Mo'
Pete Brookes
Roger Thomas Brooks
Stephen Broomhall
Ally Brown
Tony Brown
Suzanne and Kristopher Bryant
Peter Burford
Daryl Burgess
Paul Burgwin
Carl Burley
Clive Burley
Ann and Ken Burton
Frank Burton
Raymond Burton
Alex Butler
Dave Butler
Alan Bynion

Chris Cadman
Jim Cadman
Sylvia and Terry Calloway
A E Campbell and N Campbell
Len Cantello
Neal Carr
Matthew Carter
The Carter Family
Andy Cartwright
Ian Cartwright
Dave Challinor
David Challinor
Richard Cheeseman

Adam Chew
Ron Chew
Conrad Chircop
Bryn Clark
Neil Clark
Darren Clarke
Dennis Clarke
Jay Claverley
John Clements
Jay Cleverley
James Coleman
Bruce Collard
Paul Collins
Ted Connop
Jeremy Cooke
Corky
Adam Cotton
Dr Clem Cottrill
Barry Cowdrill
Dave Cox
Campbell Crawford
Nick Cross
David Crumpton
Margaret Crumpton
Martin Crumpton
Steven Crumpton
Ian 'Bluenose' Cruxton
Con Cunningham

Nigel Dale
Joe Davis
Marcus Davis
Roger Denley
David Derricott
Kevan Done
David H Donel
Steven Donnithorne
Kevin Donovan
Keith Downing
Ray Duffin
William A Dutton

Richard Eades 'aka Baggie Bird'
Suzan Eames
Jonathan Eden
Neil Edmonds
Paul Eley

Will Eley
Jeremy Elwell
Claire Evans (Wolves fan!)
Bill Evitts
Carol Ewen and Alan Yeomans
Alistair, Jenna (Faulkner),
Finley and Penny Ewen
Jack Ewen-Mountford,
Phoebe Bradd-Ewen and
Alexandra Ewen
Jo, Keith, Tayla-Mae and
Hugo Ewen

Ray Fairfax
Alan Farnell
Wayne Ferriday
Karl Fletcher
Doug Fraser
Josephine French
Kelly Louise Jackson and
Mark French
Pat Frost
Malcolm Frowen
Micky Fudge

David Garrett
Mark 'Old Fossil' Gascoigne
The Gibbard Family
Phil Gilchrist
Johnny Giles
Andy Gittins
Ray Glasby and Lynda Riley
Ann Glaze
Andrew Glazzard
Andrew, Rebecca and
Charlotte Glazzard
Ray Glazzard
Tony Godden
Jim Goode
John Goode
Don Goodman
Richard Goodwin
Zachary Goodwin
Bobby Gould
Dave Grady
Martin Grange
Chloe Elizabeth Grant

186

David Grant
Peter A Grant
In memory of Ralph Graves
Les Green
Teresa, Chris and Nicholas Green
Mel Greenfield
Mark Grew
Ray Grice
David Griffiths
Tony Griffiths
Jordan Grigg
Tracey Guthrie

Gary Hackett
Richard Haddlesey
Dave Hadley
Ian Hamilton
Michael Handley
Barry Harris
Harry Harris
Mick Harrison
John Hartson
David Hawkins
Jenny and Martin Hawkins
Mattie Hawkins
Richard Hawkins
Amanda Hayden
Barbara Hayden
Roy Hayden
Charles Haynes
Gavin Haynes
Jon Haynes
Ashley Hayward
Rob Henderson
Terry Henderson
Daniel Hewitt
Mark Hewitt
Phil and Di Hewitt
John Hickman
Jodee Ann Hill
Wain Hinton
Shaun Hinton
Ken Hodgkisson
Linda Holder 'Lyn'
Andy Hollis
Dave Holloway
Paul Holmes

Angela Holyhead
Brian Stephen Holyhead
Brett Ryan Holyhead
Daniel Stephen Holyhead
In memory of Terence H Holyhead
Kevin Terence Holyhead
Luke Kevin Holyhead
John Homer
Paul Homer
Roger Homer
Bobby Hope
Arthur Horton
Bill Howell
Louise and Peggy Howell
In memory of Mick Howell
Graham Hubble
Andrew Hudson
Gary Hudson
Graham Hughes
Len Hughes
Des Humphries
Adam, Kate and Jack Hunter
In memory of Kevin Hunter
Marie Hutchison and Philip Morris
Roy Hunter
Sandra Hunter
Barry Hurst
Brad Hurst
Charlie Hurst
Dr Judith Hurst nee Rimmer

The Insley family, Annette,
Rob and Nick
Trevor Instone

Alec Jackson
Malcolm Jackson
Andy Johnson
Baron Johnson
Dave Johnson
Willie Johnston
Barry Jones
Bob Jones
Peter Jones
Stan Jones
Tim Jones
Trevor Richard Jordan

John Kaye
Zahra, Hannah and Amelia Khan
Steve Killworth
Philip Kingston
Chris Kinsey

The Laird family
Andrew Lambourn
Roy Lander
Graham Large
David Law
Keith Law
Trevor Law
Carl Lawley
Chris Lepkowski
Paul Lester
Steve Lilwall
Margaret Limbrick
Derek Linney
John Lovatt
Matt Love
Graham Lovett
Tony Lloyd
Sean Lynch

Eric MacDonald
Rachael Machin
Colin Mackenzie
Lachlan Macpherson
John Maddocks
Brian and Diane Male
Spiro Marcetic
Paul Mardon
Barry Marsh
Mick Martin
Val Martin
Alex, Deborah, Evie and
Lois Matthews
Christine Matthews
Ivan, Jane and Sophie Matthews
Joe Mayo
Mike McCannon
Evlyne McConigley
Billy McDonald
Rita McLaughlan
Duncan Mcloud
Bernard McNally

Iain McPheely
Albert McPherson
Tracey Mee
David Meese
Elliott Meese
Jonathan Meese
Richard Meese
Alan Merrick
Andy Miles
Stuart Miller
Jonathan Millership
Roy Millership
Derek Monaghan
Darren Moore
John More
Dave Morgan
Roy Morley
Gary Morton
Tony Mowbray
Andrew Mullins
Dee Murphy
Ian Murphy
Steve Murphy

Stuart Naylor
Tom and Chris Newey
Gordon Nisbet

Adrian O'Donnell and
Wendy Vaughan
Michael and Lesley O'Donnell
Richard O'Kelly
Mike O'Leary
Edward O'Quinn-Morris
Bernard Orme
Alan Owen
Gary Owen

Darren Parsons
Peter Parsons
Patch Partridge
In memory of Alfred Jim Payne
Richard Payne
Ian Payton
Garth Pearce
Bailey and Jake Pearson
Richard Perkins

Michael Perry
Susie Peters
Deb Phillips
Stewart Phillips
Trevor Phillips
Richard Pierce
Alan Pierdziwol
Roger Pitt
Tony Potter
Kevin Price
Luke Price
John Prince
Mitch Pryce

Richard Ralphs
Darren Rampling
Laurie Rampling
Bill Rana
Andy Randon
Dave Randon
Paul Raven
Mark Ray
Phil Reade
Cyrille Regis MBE
Neal Reynolds
Neil Reynolds
Daniel Richards
Dr Roger Rimmer
John Rimmer
Phil Rimmer
Richard Roberts
Ally Robertson
James Robinson
Keith Robinson
Wendy and Mike Robinson
Bryan Robson
Michael Rodosthenous
Chris Room
Tom Ross
Jon Round
Denis Ruby
John Russell
Jonathan Russell
Kev Ruston

Pete Sargent
David Seal

Craig Shakespeare
Steve Shore
Steve Sidaway
Graham Hampson Silk
John Simpson
John Charles Simpson
Marc Sinfield
Mark Skipton
Geoff Slater
John Slater
Paul Slater
Gavin Sloan
Bill Smith
Kenneth Smith
Margi Smith
Matthew Smith
Maurice Smith
Neil Smith
Dale Smyth
Paul Smyth
Geoff Snape
Richard Sneekes
John Southwick
Derek Spires
Ashley Starbuck
Derek Statham
Gary Strodder
Roger and Beth Stubbs
Colin Suggett
Amy Sunburk
Charlotte Sunburk
David Sunburk
Helen and Martin Sunburk
Bernadette and Dave Swanwick
Robert Swanwick
Deborah Swanwick-Baker and
Matthew Baker

Brian Talbot
Alan Taylor
Barry Taylor
Bob Taylor
Brian Taylor
Chris and Brandon Taylor
Darrell Taylor
James Taylor
Kevin Taylor

Catherine Terry
Paul Thompson
Steve Thompson
Chris Thornton
Mike Tilt
Tony Timmins
Nikki Timmis
Laura Todd
John Trewick
Simon Trigg
John, Helen and
Elizabeth Tromans
Judith and Noel Tumelty
Lillian Turner
Peter Turner
Roger Turner
John V Tuzzio

Elliot and Lily Upton

Bev, Nathan and Matthew Veness
Mark Venus
John Viveash

WBAFPA
WBA SC Kidderminster
Dr Peter J Wagstaff
Charles Waldock
Dean Walton
Robert Waterhouse
Tom Waterhouse
David J Watkin
Dougie Webb
Jez Webb
Margaret Webster
Bob Weeks
Norman Westbury
George Wheatley
Keith Wheeler
Clive Whitehead
Brenda and Mike Whitehouse
Brian Whitehouse
Geoffrey and Andrew Whitehouse
Mark Snarka Whitehouse
Malcolm Wilcox
Tom Wilcox
John Wile

Graham Williams
Brian Willis
Colin Wills
James Wills
Terry Wills
Ray Wilson
Ken Winning
Sarah Winning
Andrew Woodall
Ian Woodward
Stewart Woolgar
Richard Woodward
Roy Woodward
Nick Worth

Acknowledgements

The publishers wish to thank everyone who has contributed to this book. Dave Matthews would have been so proud – it has been a real team effort.

In particular, we would like to acknowledge Albion's ever-cheerful club photographer Laurie Rampling for supplying not only the excellent photos for the front and back covers but also more than a few of those on the inside pages. If we have inadvertently breached copyright issues with the use of any of the others, please let us know so we can address this matter.

We are also extremely grateful to Steve Gordos, himself an accomplished author, for the diligence and speed of his proof reading and to the considerable number of friends who have become supporters and/or sellers of this publication. Top of the table in this respect has to be the club's Former Players Association. How lovely it is to see so many Hawthorns favourites among the subscribers. The Supporters Club, in particular those from the Kidderminster branch, have been extremely generous, too.

Finally, to Albion themselves, who Dave was proud to work for more than half a century, we extend our gratitude for their full cooperation and backing.